For
Men
Only

ALSO BY GERALD IMBER, M.D.

The Youth Corridor: A Renowned Plastic Surgeon's Revolutionary Program for Maintenance, Rejuvenation, and Timeless Beauty

For Men Only

Looking Your Best Through Science, Surgery, and Common Sense

Gerald Imber, M.D.

WILLIAM MORROW AND COMPANY, INC.
NEW YORK

It is the policy of William Morrow and Company, Inc., and its imprints and affiliates, recognizing the
importance of preserving what has been written, to print the books we publish on acid-free paper,
and we exert our best efforts to that end.

Library of Congress Cataloging-in-Publication Data

Imber, Gerald.
For men only : looking your best through science, surgery, and
common sense / by Gerald Imber.
p.   cm.
ISBN 0-688-15800-5 (alk. paper)
1. Men—Health and hygiene—Popular works.   2. Skin—Aging—
Popular works.   3. Skin—Care and hygiene—Popular works.
4. Beauty, Personal.   I. Title.
RA777.8.I43   1998
613'.04234—dc21   98-29411
CIP

Printed in the United States of America

First Edition

1 2 3 4 5 6 7 8 9 10

BOOK DESIGN BY RENATO STANISIC

www.williammorrow.com

FOR JOEL,
whose year has been a mirror of life itself

Acknowledgments

This volume owes its existence to the commitment of everyone concerned with *The Youth Corridor,* both as a book and as a way of life—those who encouraged the writing, and those who daily help me help our patients. The idea of youth maintenance by lifestyle alteration and the use of smaller, less invasive procedures, performed earlier in life, has proven its worth. More people are able to keep their vital good looks longer and without waiting for drastic changes to become necessary.

Here, we are going a step further. We are attempting to provide the first men's guide to looking one's best and controlling the effects of aging. This is no small task, for men's interests have been long ignored and there is more to say than space allows.

Many people have helped: Katey Langer, who helped juggle my hats (as usual), Myrna Laureano, Denise Swanzey, and Kelly Greenlaw, among others, who kept the office working smoothly. Lila J. Landé, who did an excellent job of research. Elizabeth Kaplan, my agent, and Claire Wachtel, my editor, who believed in the need for this book. And Cathryn Collins, who, as always, has supported me wholeheartedly through this project with intelligent advice and good judgment.

Contents

Introduction

Not very long ago I had the opportunity to publish my strategies for the maintenance of youthful good looks. Although a great deal of the information in *The Youth Corridor* applied to everyone, it was primarily organized to address issues facing women. Why? Because that's who pores over the beauty articles featured in every magazine. That's who keeps a billion-dollar cosmetics and skin care industry humming, that's who we thought would be most interested, would listen to sound advice, and would buy the book. And women did listen. They bought the book, and they learned from the routines I had been offering my patients for years, and they were able to help themselves. That, of course, was very gratifying, if predictable.

Early in the life of the book, a bookstore operator from a large southern city visited my office in New York for a consultation. The consultation was followed by a pleasant chat, during which I spoke of the possibility of a book for men. As has been the case since the inception of the idea, I found it immediately necessary to defend the project with my usual comment: "Men are every bit as interested in their appearance as women." I wasn't more than a few seconds into an often-repeated routine when she gracefully interrupted.

"You are so right," she said. "I always knew which car my ex-husband had last used just from looking at the position of the mirror. He invariably turned it down to look at himself before stepping out."

That pretty much makes my argument. The simple truth is that men are every bit as self-aware as women, and every bit as vain. The issues and the standards against which we judge ourselves may be different, but the basic instinct is the same. Gray hair and smile lines

have a different significance and may not be as disturbing to us as they are to women, but we too stare at the mirror. We may do our staring with the door closed, but stare we do.

The July 2, 1997, edition of the *International Herald Tribune* featured a story on grooming, which opened, "Summer is here, the beach beckons, and the Parisian man's thoughts turn to getting his chest hair dyed." That certainly is not what this book is about. It represents one end of the spectrum of self-interest and vanity, perhaps balancing those men on the other end who actually make no effort toward maximizing their appearance and maintaining their youth. For most of us, reality is somewhere in the middle. Fashion and fitness have crossed all cultural borders. Though the majority of men have not yet become prey to the cult of cosmetics, there is a growing male market in ethical and effective skin care products. The gym is full of men of all ages, lifestyles, and professions who do care, and these days the reason real men don't eat quiche is that it is made of eggs. Men are eating salads, pasta, and vegetables more often and red meat far less often than in the past. They have stopped smoking and they drink less, and the only drug in sight is an aspirin as a strategy against heart attack. In short, men are concerned with their health and their appearance. They are concerned with the signs of aging, and concerned that they don't seem overly concerned. That too is changing, and there is an urgent, and unmet, hunger for information.

The goal of this book is to help you look your best forever. An ambitious goal indeed. To accomplish it I will provide a comprehensive source for the latest scientific antiaging strategies, preventive and maintenance routines, and the full menu of corrective measures—everything necessary to keep you looking your youthful best.

Men require a convenient source for this information, and it is nowhere to be found. Women, however, have had the benefit of decades of journalistic advice culled from the fringes, if not the core, of science. These ubiquitous pieces have dealt with issues of health, beauty, fitness, and, more recently, youth maintenance and sexuality. The nature of periodicals precludes the issues being covered in depth, and worst of all, from the man's point of view, they are aimed at women and published primarily in fashion magazines and the "ladies' press." More important than anatomical variation is the different emphasis the sexes place on specific changes, and these must be taken into account. The health information in fashion magazines is not wholly applicable to men. Still, similar forums for dissemination of appropriate information to men have not existed until recently and not nearly on the same scale.

Men's magazines have been around forever, but their thrust (perhaps a very appropriate word indeed) has been of a far different nature. For more than a hundred years these journals have survived on tales of hypermasculinity in the face of conflict—conflict with the perils of war, the great outdoors, the dark spectrum of crime, and, most of all, the female. It's an old story, and dreams have always been great sellers. Little difference exists between the artificial sexuality of *Playboy* and *Penthouse* and the man-against-grizzly stories in the gun magazines. All pander to fantasies of idealized masculinity, devoid of introspection, weakness, or reality. In other words, they don't help the average guy cope. Most women's magazines have had at least a secondary mission to provide help with the reality of modern life. The men's magazines that have seen the light have done very well indeed. Again, a testimonial to the need for information.

Until recently, men seem to have taken all of this in stride. Our problems and our secrets were our own . . . which is not all bad. Certainly no one wants to be bothered with a whiny man, constantly letting it all hang out, but that too is a caricature. True, success and power are potent aphrodisiacs, and if that's all you have, use it. Secret dreams and aspirations rarely have money as their central focus. Men do care about more than success and performance in the marketplace, and if they are not as sensitive and open as women, that is reality. Despite assumptions to the contrary, men are deeply concerned with their appearance, and this even before the specter of aging raises its gray head. The concern takes different forms from the female variety, and all but the most liberated, or obsessed, among us have embraced some element of feigned indifference that society has deemed appropriate. We care about the way we look to ourselves, to women, and to other men. We care deeply about sexual perception and performance and the projection of vitality and power. There are very few exceptions. The pipe-smoking professor in his scruffy cardigan and tweeds has made decisions about his place and image, even if that image takes the form of rejection of convention; in some circles, it may be convention itself. The point is, we all care a great deal about our appearance. We may not feel the need to have abs of steel, but we want to look healthy, powerful, and attractive. And we want to maintain our youthful good looks for at least as long as we feel a part of the vital life around us.

This book will focus on those aspects of appearance, face and body, that can be positively influenced. If we can't do anything about it, we won't waste time wringing our hands. Rather, we will get on to areas where we can help ourselves. Self-diagnosis is the

step before self-help, and self-help is the basic fabric of an effort such as this. Both will be dealt with in depth. Where professional intervention is the only choice, the options will be fully explored. The objective is to help you do the best for yourself, feel good about it, and get the most out of life.

Understanding what it takes to look good involves more than a litany about skin care, aging prevention, and cosmetic surgery. It must focus on the elements of appearance that concern men, how they change through life, and how one's physical appearance may be influenced, controlled, and altered. That is an important task, and one that I have taken seriously for more than two decades of professional practice. This book will offer much of the information I have compiled over the years, and a complete overview both of what you can do for yourself and of what plastic surgeons can do for you.

In many respects, this book is about aging, for so much changes with the years that we must become aware of the insidious, imperceptible daily changes and stop them before the damage is done. This must be dealt with earlier rather than later. Unfortunately, those young enough to influence and control aging most easily have virtually no interest in the topic. Men particularly have to see the first signs of aging before the topic becomes real. To fully understand this we will explore how the skin ages, how that aging is manifested in our appearance, and how to use this knowledge to prevent and reverse these effects of aging.

In some ways men manifest signs of aging differently from women, and, more significant, they react differently to the various signs. For example, men rarely give a second thought to frown lines, but the same men will be extremely sensitive to loose neck skin, baggy eyes, and hair loss. With that in mind, our point of view will be exclusively male.

The changes that bother us are unwelcome because they are all too closely identified with a conceptual loss of vitality, virility, and power. So we work out, but can't work off those "love handles." We watch our diet, and still our bodies change. We drink less and sleep more, and yet we have bags beneath our eyes. And on and on.

All these are real issues, some shared with women, some exclusively ours. As a group, men are not particularly concerned with wrinkles. Not for some stoic reason, but because our anatomy differs significantly from that of women, specifically in the presence of the thick skin and rich blood supply that sustains the beard, and because of daily shaving, which acts as an exfoliant. Thus wrinkled skin is less of an issue for us than it is for women. You will understand more of this as we explore the conditions of aging and pre-

vention of aging in greater depth. You will understand the changes of aging and how each develops. You will learn how to prevent these changes, how to arrest them, and how to reverse them. You will learn how to recognize your own problems and those of others, and what is available for their control and correction. The age-specific program provided will clearly define the proper routine for each individual at each stage of life.

When you finish reading this book, you will have been introduced to the full spectrum of prevention, maintenance, and correction, and you will be able to exert a positive influence on how you look and how you age. With little effort you can look your best at every stage of life. Though you cannot yet stop aging, there is much you can do to influence it, and, more important, you can learn to stop exerting negative influences on your appearance and begin to help yourself.

The idea is to maintain an attractive and youthful appearance throughout the adult years. It is possible, and this book will help you do it.

For Men Only

Growing Up and Growing Old

Reality is knocking at the door. In the physiological sense, growing up means little more than the beginning of the downslide. There is no point in time when the pinnacle of mature adulthood is reached . . . and stands still. From birth to death, a long-term status quo is never achieved. In fact, in the average life span of nearly fourscore years, we spend the last sixty undoing the first twenty. This doesn't refer to the oddity of the professional athlete truly wearing out the ligaments and cartilage of his back and knees and elbows from excessive and unnatural wear and tear. At age thirty, Boris Becker reached the end of the line in big-time tennis. The "clean living" abuse to his body had accelerated the skeletal aging process beyond competitive tolerance. This, of course, is an exceptional case, but it makes the point. There is a finite life span inherent in the genetic code of human tissues. A predetermined number of cell turnovers, repairs, and replications can take place before breakdown, disease, and ultimately shutdown begin. This gloomy fact has led the scientific community to many interesting approaches to individual tissue and ultimately whole-body longevity. Studies of genetics and cellular biology have identified the areas susceptible to wearing out and are on the verge of controlling the process. Though all this is tomorrow's news, it has profound application to today's living.

The lesson is that even when cellular longevity can be achieved, it cannot undo failed systems. For the most part, when the damage is done, the damage is done. After a certain level of destruction, organs cannot regenerate. The more critical the organ, the greater effect on the body as a whole. For today, the philosophy is to protect what you have. This applies to the body as a whole, although the effect of aging processes upon the skin may in some measure be reversible. Most of the issues we will explore pertain to the skin in particular, as that is the mirror of the aging process and the indelible evidence that we must face. However, it is imperative to understand that the skin is, in many ways, a reflection of the general health of the body as a whole. Though many conditions and situations exist that affect the aging process of the skin alone, one should not minimize the importance of overall good health, or its absence. Systemic illnesses have enormous impact on the aging process, and therefore on one's appearance. For example, the hormone insulin is manufactured in the pancreas, and is largely responsible for sugar metabolism. Diminished quantities of insulin result in the metabolic disease known as diabetes. Therefore, sugar intolerance has become synonymous with diabetes. Numerous other aspects of the disease are also well known, among them the causal relationship between diabetes and impaired small vessel blood flow, and its effects are far-reaching, sparing no system. Among the least threatening of these possibilities is the effect of diabetes upon the small blood vessels nourishing the skin, but this illustrates an important point. Reduced blood flow through the small vessels of the skin results in reduced nutrient supply to the tissue and impaired removal of metabolic wastes, contributing to loss of elasticity, thinning of the basal cell layer, oxidation and thinning of the collagen layer, and wrinkling. In other words, diabetes causes premature aging of the skin.

Obviously, this is not the most worrisome effect of diabetes, but it serves to illustrate how important the overall state of health is in determining how one's skin, and therefore one's appearance, will fare over the years.

Most of the external forces responsible for the acceleration of visible aging are those that act directly on the skin itself. These are important and obvious, and we must be certain not to underestimate the importance of both one's general health and those specific circumstances that exert significant influence upon one's appearance. In many ways the state of aging is a manifestation of the general condition of the individual, and we will pay proper respect and attention here, even while we concentrate on maximizing one's outward appearance and the control and reversal of the signs of aging.

Is this attitude superficial? Indeed it is, and if you truly believe that the way you look is unimportant, stop reading now. The importance of looking good is reality. Should it be so important? Perhaps not. But our task is to live happily and successfully and constructively in the world as we have found it. Appearance is important. It allows us the opportunity to strut our stuff and let people know how really good we are. It opens the door, and not only in the social sense. It is a fact of life that if two candidates, equally qualified in all other respects, are seeking the same position, an employer will automatically gravitate to the more physically attractive person. That is the definition of attractive. Certainly an unlikely and extreme example to illustrate the point, but like it or not, this is the way things are, and we must deal with reality. Make the most of your appearance, and your life, and if you think all of this is unfair, change society along the way. These ubiquitous societal pressures have been around throughout recorded history. They may vary from culture to culture, but you might just as well resign yourself to doing your best within the existing structure. It is not about to change, and it is pointless to sit around whining when there's a job to be done. That job is to be the best you possibly can. Will all this bring happiness? In many ways, yes. It will allow you to look your best, feel better about yourself, and begin a cycle of improvement and achievement that can be at the very heart of happiness, and that's a pretty lofty goal.

My professional concern has always been to minimize defects and maximize an individual's appearance. This pertains to cancer care and reconstruction as well as to antiaging and other cosmetic surgery. Regard for the form of the individual, and not solely function, is a distinguishing trait that sets the plastic surgeon apart from his medical colleagues. All this concern for appearance must occur within the bounds of common sense and reason, for though we are devoted to maintaining and maximizing appearance, it must not be at the expense of a natural self-restraint. Obvious signs of plastic surgery, such as hair transplants that look like a stand of trees or any feature that is so unnatural or out of place that it doesn't fit the environment, defeat the purpose. The objective is to be vital, look youthful, look good, and look natural. Anything less is a waste of time, effort, and money!

In the following chapters of this book, I will cover the science of aging and its practical implications. This book must focus around measures to identify troubling changes and stop or correct them, but the bigger picture in antiaging science is the coming revolution in gene therapy, which will rapidly reverse most visible manifestations of aging. Coming soon to a doctor's office near you? Not quite. But it is real, and it is on the way. Meanwhile we will continue to perfect maintenance and corrective measures to keep you at your best until that day comes.

HOW WE AGE

This is a topic that starts with the very basics of cell biology. Without some rudimentary knowledge of the process we can understand neither the changes we see nor the importance of recent advances in their control, to say nothing of the fantastic changes barely over the horizon. From our selfish perspective we are interested solely in what all this can do to increase our longevity and keep us looking young. And that is a legitimate perspective. But we must first define what has been happening and what changes are actually attributable to the process.

The functioning parts of the human body are composed of cells. They may be bathed in inert fluids, deposit inactive materials, and excrete nonviable wastes, but the woven tissues of living cells and the isolated nomadic cells of the blood share the responsibility for sustaining life. They also share a planned obsolescence. The genetic matter of each cell, separately encoded with information in the form of paired protein bases, is charged with the responsibility of passing on this master plan to its next generation of replacements. In principle, as each cell wears out it is replaced by an exact duplicate carrying the same genetic messages in its chromosomes, and therefore is capable of smoothly transferring the duties of the tissues.

This would go on indefinitely if the plan were so simple. Unfortunately, a number of significant changes occur with time. There actually seems to be a shortening of a protein at the end of each chromosome with each replication. This portion is called the telomere. When it is shortened beyond a critical point, the replicated chromosome is deficient; the cell slows down and ultimately becomes unable to reproduce itself. This is, at the most basic level, the aging of the cell.

When cells are unable to function and reproduce themselves, the amassed unit of cells, or tissue, can no longer perform its duties. It ages. It becomes inefficient and ultimately ceases to function. When the ability to function crosses a critical threshold and an important organ ceases functioning, the entire organism is at risk of dying. In fact, excepting accident and disease, this is death from natural causes. Obviously, we want to keep it all at bay as long as possible. Keep those cells turning over quickly. Keep them working and replicating, and keep us young and keep us alive.

An excellent plan. Unfortunately, cells can turn over only a finite number of times. This limited ability of cell replication actually has a name, the **Hayflick number**, for Leonard Hayflick, the scientist who broke the bad news. The Hayflick number represents the number of divisions possible by a particular type of cell before it exhausts its ability to replicate itself and succumbs, leading to tissue and organ destruction in succession. Cellular mortality is the story of human mortality, and understanding the process is crucial to doing something about it.

This finite ability of cellular reproduction is intimately related to telomere shortening, and should be kept in mind. It will play a great role in our future, and our not too distant future at that. We will explore this later, and those with deeper interest will be fascinated by a book called *Reversing Human Aging* by Dr. Michael Fossel (Morrow, 1996), which covers the subject expertly and in some depth.

For this discussion we must be aware that the Hayflick number is limiting the number of replacement cells we can produce, so if we want to be around and functioning well, we had better protect the ones we have. In large part, that is what this book is about. Soon science will be available to suspend aging and prolong life beyond our dreams, but for the most part this will benefit only undamaged tissue and organs. There is nothing on the practical or theoretical horizon that will reverse damage to heart muscle or failing kidneys, so we must do whatever is within our power to prevent these catastrophic occurrences if we are to take advantage of what medical science will offer.

The skin, however, represents a slightly different circumstance. Here, by voiding the Hayflick limit on cell turnover and encouraging rapid turnover and youthful cellular activity, science can revitalize the entire organ known as skin. This is because no life-sustaining functions have been shut down. In fact, none reside here. As important as the skin is in bodily function, it ages in a manner indicative of decreased vitality, sort of a mirror of what is happening inside. The skin thins as collagen fibers become fewer and less well aligned. Surface cells pile up irregularly, the basal layer flattens and diminishes, the skin becomes dry, fewer elastin fibers are manufactured, others are destroyed, and the skin becomes loose. In other words, it ages.

In January 1998 the first word of genetically induced telomere lengthening in human cells was reported in newspapers around the world. By altering the genes of cells, scientists were able to induce the production of telomerase, the enzyme responsible for maintaining telomere length. Theoretically, this will allow infinite cell replications. This is good news for aging skin, for these changes will very likely be among the first amenable to chromosome manipulation. Increased cellular activity will result in greater and more orderly collagen and elastin production, finer and better-lubricated skin surface, and ultimately healthier, better-fitting, more youthful skin. The fact that skin changes will be reversible should come as little surprise to students of the aging process, as we are even now able to exert some effect on the process. More about that later—now it will be enough to know that in a limited way we can reverse skin damage, and should soon make far greater strides in that direction.

THE STRUCTURE OF SKIN

Human skin is a functioning organ weighing some ten pounds in the average male. It is made up of an outer layer, the **epidermis,** and a deeper layer, the **dermis.** The epidermis is what we see. The skin presents itself to public view in the form of the **stratum corneum,** the multilayered zone of dead cells above the basal layer of the epidermis. This basal layer is virtually the only living part of the epidermis, and it manufactures cells called **keratinocytes,** which work their way to the surface of the skin. Here the keratinocytes are gradually transformed into a protective layer of dead cells, called the **keratinized layer,** or stratum corneum. The actual look and feel of the skin reflects the condition of this layer. An irregular skin surface is due to the presence of heaped-up keratinized cells in this outer layer, which have not been shed in the regular pattern of youthful skin. It shows wrinkles, gets sunburned, and becomes scaly, discolored, blotchy, or dry when not properly cared for. As the skin ages, far more care is necessary to preserve the same state of well-being that comes naturally with youth. Dry skin is the result of poor hydration of these dead cells. Important as it is, the epidermis alone does not fully determine the appearance of the skin, but it is the presenting part and always on display.

The dermis is made up of several elements. It contains living cells as well as the primary structural element of the skin, **collagen.** This is an organized layer of parallel microscopic bands of chemically linked amino acids. The collagen layer is usually somewhat thicker in men than in women, and it varies with skin type and age. Combined with the collagen is a similar substance called **elastin,** which gives the skin its resilience. Collagen and elastin are very crucial elements, for they provide the skin tone and elasticity that define a youthful and attractive appearance. The skin will function perfectly well in its role as gatekeeper, keeping body fluids in and the external environment out, even with degenerated, loose, thinned collagen, but it certainly won't look good doing it. The collagen layer of the dermis is the source of the wrinkles seen on the epidermal surface.

Within the dermis are the blood vessels of the skin, as well as the sweat and oil glands,

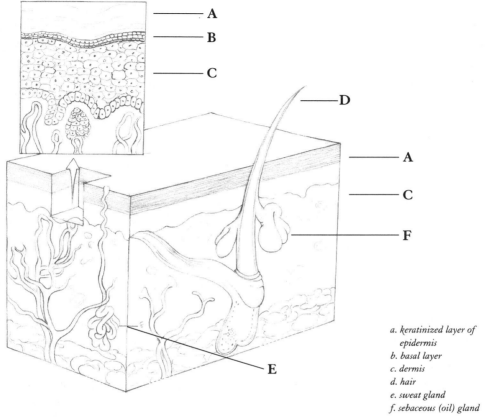

A
B
C
D
A
C
F
E

a. keratinized layer of
   epidermis
b. basal layer
c. dermis
d. hair
e. sweat gland
f. sebaceous (oil) gland

Stylized microscopic view of a cross section through human skin

which lubricate the skin and regulate internal body temperature. These functions, regulating body temperature and separating internal from external environment, are what make the skin an important organ. Sweat glands are a primary method of releasing heat from an overheated body by secreting water, which evaporates on the skin surface and cools the body as the blood vessels dilate and present more blood near the surface for cooling. In frigid situations where heat conservation is necessary, the sweat glands don't secrete and the blood vessels in the skin constrict so that minimal heat is lost.

Beneath the dermis is the superficial fatty layer of the skin. This too is an integral part of the skin and contains many of the elements that serve the skin, such as blood vessels and nerve fibers.

How Skin Is Damaged

A great deal of this anatomy lesson has practical application beyond the discussion of aging. Simple wounds are an excellent example. A paper cut that opens the skin but doesn't bleed is an epidermal wound. Easy to understand, since the epidermis has no significant blood vessels. A cut that bleeds is into the dermis, for that is where the blood vessels reside. A wound that gapes open is usually through the dermis and into the subdermal fat. This represents a wound merely a fraction of an inch deep, since the thickness of the epidermis and dermis combined is less than a tenth of an inch.

The redness of sunburn is an injury to the epidermis. Peeling skin, which results from the injury, is the loss of epidermis. These are not dangerous injuries in the immediate sense, as the skin will immediately regenerate. The true danger in repeated superficial burn injuries is in the increased likelihood of skin cancers. Deeper burns, even second-degree sunburns, are into the dermis. These usually heal and look normal, though the risk of skin cancer further increases. Third-degree burns destroy the dermis and the glands from which the skin would regenerate. These burns result in scars, not skin.

Wrinkles are the result of several factors. If one thinks of the skin repeatedly folding and unfolding in a place determined by muscle action, like the inner surface of the elbow or smile lines alongside the eyes, it is as easy to picture the collagen breaking down and forming permanent lines, or wrinkles, as it is to predict the breakdown of a piece of cardboard folded and refolded in the same place. Irreparable damage has been done to the cardboard. The same thing happens with skin, though some of the damage may be undone. The other, more insidious way for wrinkles to develop is through chemical oxidation of the collagen fibers. This can be the work of circulating free radicals. These are single, unpaired molecules of oxygen, not in the stable O_2 state we usually assume. The circulating free radicals bind to the collagen and oxidize and denature it. The action of ultraviolet light upon the skin accelerates this form of collagen breakdown, by accelerating free radical production. Whatever the cause, it is this disruption of collagen from its healthy, finely organized state that results in dermal wrinkles, then reflected in the epidermis, which is ever so closely bonded to the dermis and mimics its defects.

Damage to the elastic fibers occurs in a similar fashion, whether through chemical or mechanical means, and is hastened by exposure to ultraviolet light. Think of your skin as a form-fitting garment, like a pair of long johns. When they are new they hug your body and move with you like a second skin. After years of service, multiple washings, and thousands of folds, the fabric begins to sag at the joints and generally loosen all over. Sadly, that is pretty much what happens to your skin. Think about this unpleasant analogy the next time you see a man with a loose "turkey gobbler" neck or saggy eyelids.

Disease states aside, the way we live affects our skin and our appearance. There is much you can do to avoid making things worse, and in fact to actually improve the situation. It is necessary to get the bad news first. Consider this a wake-up call.

HOW AGING AFFECTS THE FACE

Now that we have shared the basic bad news about the process of aging, it is time to deal in specifics. The culprits have been identified as wear and tear of the years, the pull of gravity against the elastic fibers, chemical denaturing, and ultraviolet damage. These changes begin very early in life but for the first two or three decades are not particularly noticeable. This is the optimal time for preventive action, which we will discuss in detail. Unfortunately for those of us no longer in our twenties, the results of these forces have already become evident. Though this damage varies with age, skin type, and lifestyle, the starting points are predictable. Even men in their mid-twenties can see early changes, though they are not yet sensitized enough to take them seriously. Changes usually begin about the eyelids, the thinnest skin of the face. Not only is this the finest skin, it also must withstand the constant motion of smiling, squinting, and frowning. It is prone to swelling in response to allergy, food intake, and emotion, and is stretched out of shape on a regular basis.

In youth the skin is quite elastic and bounces back without difficulty. Even while this resilient state persists, the constant motion begins to etch the earliest lines alongside the eyes and beneath them. This usually becomes noticeable around age thirty. The changes soon progress to slightly loosened skin of the upper lids, then puffiness of the lower lids. All the while the lines continue to deepen and extend. By forty-five to fifty these changes have become fully developed, and there is excess skin on the upper lids and baggy skin on the lowers, and the wrinkles have become more numerous and deeper.

Other changes begin concomitantly, but are manifested later than changes around the eyes. These include deepening of the nasolabial line, which courses from the out-

What you look like at age twenty-five

What you look like at age thirty-five

What you look like at age forty-five

What you look like at age fifty-five

side of the nose to the corners of the mouth. The line increases in depth over the years and by fifty is fully developed into a fold with a permanent line etched in the bottom. Later this process proceeds to jowls, which cross the jawline accompanied by loose skin of the neck, becoming increasingly obvious with time. Vertical frown lines develop between the eyebrows at different times of life. This depends upon one's facial musculature and tendency to inadvertent frowning. Thinning of hair begins in the twenties and proceeds in male-pattern hair loss, which is usually maximal by age fifty and then levels off. Horizontal furrows develop in the forehead and continue to deepen. Eyelid skin becomes more redundant, dark spots develop on the cheeks and forehead, and skin becomes increasingly dry. Some superficial wrinkling develops, small superficial capillaries on sides of nose and cheeks.

What you look like at age sixty-five

This pattern of aging differs from that seen in women. Men rarely have significant wrinkling of the cheeks, or vertical lines of the upper lip, though a more pronounced accumulation of loose skin beneath the jaw and on the neck is the rule.

The five illustrations on pages 10 and 11 depict a male face from about age twenty-five to about age sixty-five, with the changes manifested in each decade. Later in life one can expect more of the same, but few new surprises. It is important to remember that the timing and intensity of these changes varies from man to man depending on numerous factors, the most important of which are heredity and lifestyle. One's aging pattern can often be predicted simply by glancing at the family album, but again, what we do and don't do greatly affects the process. These illustrations are simply an overview, though for most of us they are not far from reality.

Heredity alone will not necessarily drive men to age in this manner. One can control the process by lifestyle alterations and self-help, and the remaining problems, if they develop, are amenable to correction by cosmetic surgery. The next logical step is to explore what is available to control the process of facial aging.

Preventive Maintenance

The idea of preventing the visible signs of facial aging, and perhaps even the actual physiological process, is, surprisingly, as new to physicians involved in the discipline as it is to you. We have learned a great deal in the last ten years, and the future looks better still. Even now we have the opportunity to take advantage of information that will truly make a difference. This was not possible only a few years ago, and we are still sorting through each new bit of information, trying to assess its full importance.

There is no place for fads and old wives' tales in serious medicine, though they are often found to have more than a grain of truth at their center. For this book and in my practice, I choose to let others try every unproven procedure and concoction. These are not good enough for my patients, and they're not good enough for you. To the extent that my knowledge and research can assure it, the advice you find here will be based on the best medical evidence, from the best sources, with historically reproducible results wherever possible. There is so much hokum being offered today, by renegade practitioners and "healers," of which we must beware. A medical degree no longer seems to guarantee thoughtful, scientific practice, and even well-educated people are eschewing conventional treatment in favor of natural and alternative treatment, using anecdotal evidence alone as justification. Well . . . some such treatments may turn out to be valid. If so, they will stand up to scientific analysis and the test of time. More than once the medical establishment, stricken with characteristic hubris, has refused to consider treatment options embraced by the public at large.

The point is, we must not reinvent the wheel at every turn. Good strategies will survive scrutiny. Most alternative treatments are well-meaning nonsense; some are misleading, and some are grossly exploitive. We are all quite gullible where miracle cures are concerned, and appearance and aging are high on the list of emotionally charged concerns. Generations of women bought every promise of age-reversal magic the cosmetics industry could dish out—bought it emotionally, intellectually, and financially, despite repeated disappointments. The only beneficiary was the cosmetics industry, but happily, even that is changing.

Still, there is another side to the coin, and that is well illustrated by the attitude many of us, myself included, took toward the use of vitamin E supplements. For many years, there had been a constant stream of propaganda about the benefits of vitamin E. Largely this was the mantra of health food enthusiasts who knew little of science and less of health. The claims were laughable and totally unsubstantiated. Improve your sexual performance, stop aging, prevent cancer, have more beautiful skin, and undergo surgery without scars. A crock of nonsense. Or was it? It turns out that extensive research at reputable institutions has given vitamin E the stamp of approval, and it stands in the forefront of antioxidant therapy recommended so strongly by concerned practitioners, including me. Why the change of heart? Because now there is scientific evidence, not hearsay and folktales, supporting the positive effects of vitamin E.

Not every claim about vitamin E has been borne out by research done thus far, but the facts now support its use. Vitamin E is a potent antioxidant and acts, among other ways, to help prevent the formation of cholesterol plaques in arteries. Closer to home, it helps prevent collagen breakdown and premature aging of the skin. Don't get too excited. It cannot do it alone, but it helps.

The point here is that even the fads may have some merit, but we must not jump blindly onto the bandwagon, or we may fall off the other side. There are many examples, both significant and small, but in light of vitamin E, the story of beta-carotene is appropriate. This compound, closely related to vitamin A, has been almost as hot as vitamin E. There have been fewer claims, but more dramatic ones, especially about its effect of reducing cholesterol deposits in the arteries. Sound familiar? Well, beta-carotene is an antioxidant too, and is said to be very effective. Unfortunately, a federally supported 1996 study showed a virtually double mortality rate for smokers taking beta-carotene than for smokers not taking it. What, exactly, does this mean? No one is certain, but there appears to be some unexplained interaction between beta-carotene and cancer. Nothing further can be inferred as yet, but for now, the use of beta-carotene supplements is discouraged. There are enough effective antioxidants to take its place to make the possible risk unnecessary.

No sharp line can be drawn between the routines of prevention and those of maintenance. For our purposes, prevention encompasses those measures that will at the very least avoid accelerating the aging process. Naturally the very idea of prevention implies early application of the principles concerned. The younger one starts, the more significant the yield will be. Nonetheless, adopting some commonsense prevention principles will yield rich dividends at any stage of life. These are primarily lifestyle alterations. Maintenance, the step after prevention, is the process of holding the status quo by active intervention. This can take the form of skin applications, microsuction, or surgery. We will deal with the simplest measures first—those that for the most part you can do for yourself. With a combination of early prevention and minimal intervention you will be able to maintain youthful, manly good looks throughout your adult life.

The ultimate story of the aging process will be told in the genes where it originates. It appears certain that some form of gene enhancement therapy will be available within the next decade. When this passes from the experimental phase into common availability, the rules will change. Until that time, true alteration of the underlying mechanism of aging remains just beyond our grasp. We do know that much of our behavior actually accelerates the aging process, and this is surely within our control. Therefore, the first step is to eliminate the negative influences from one's lifestyle. Simultaneously, there are lifestyle alterations that will help prevent accelerated aging and actually slow down the normal process.

Some of these strategies will be well known to you, others less so. All play an important role and should be seriously considered, and adopted where applicable. None is particularly onerous. All have a significant upside, and together they present a positive step in self-help. There is no excuse for dissatisfaction with the way you look, or the way you are aging. It is very easy to do something about it. Get started. Now!

The prevention and maintenance measures discussed in this section of the book cost little in time, money, or effort, and most of them should be on every man's agenda. They include:

- Sun protection
- Antioxidant therapy
- Diet and weight control
- Exercise
- Refraining from smoking
- Use of alpha-hydroxy acid therapy
- Use of tretinoin
- Use of human growth hormone
- A daily skin care routine

All the other things we will discuss, including cosmetic surgery, come later and are for those who select them. This part of the book is for everyone.

SUN PROTECTION

Under the microscope the skin of a young adult exposed to the sun and the aging skin of an older individual share many characteristics. The basal layer of the epidermis is thinned, old cells are heaped up, not shed from the surface, and the collagen layer is thinned and disorganized. What this means is that sun exposure causes premature aging of the skin. There is simply no question about it. And premature aging takes the form of wrinkles, sagging, loose skin, blotches, and discolorations. If that were not enough, the same mechanism that causes premature aging of the skin also causes skin cancer.

Actively encouraging your skin to age, wrinkle, and sag is what you are doing when you tan. Sunburn is much worse. Every characteristic of aged skin is accelerated by those years at the beach. The damage will not be visible today or tomorrow, but a decade or two down the road. Unfortunately, our society continues to place great emphasis on the "healthy" look of a tan. We associate tan with leisure, success, and the good life. In fact, we subconsciously associate tan with good looks. That is unfortunate, but it's a fact we must live with. Remember, we don't have time to change the world, so we must adapt, and manage to live within it as well as we can. That includes limited sun exposure, dedicated use of sunblocks, and protective clothing. Can you get a little sun? Of course you can, but the damage is cumulative. It reflects the hours of modest, unremarkable exposure as well as the sunburns incurred. It is modified by the amount of melanin in the skin, and is not quite as injurious to darker people as to the very fair-skinned.

The American Academy of Dermatology states that the majority of undesirable clinical features associated with skin aging are the result of damage from ultraviolet radiation. That is, basically, ultraviolet radiation in sunlight. (Let's leave X rays and other forms of radiation aside, for they present distinct problems of their own.) Sunlight is divided into bands according to the wavelength of the light. Our primary concerns are with the bands called ultraviolet A and ultraviolet B—UVA and UVB. They are closely related, and the spectrum of one melds into the spectrum of the other.

There is far more UVA radiation in the atmosphere than there is UVB, but UVA is estimated to be only one thousandth as destructive to the skin as UVB. The less prevalent, but more destructive, UVB is responsible for the majority of sunburn, skin aging, and skin cancer. Though UVB is far more potentially dangerous, UVA too must be protected against, simply because of its prevalence.

The dangerous UVB radiation is largely absorbed by the ozone layer of the atmosphere. The ozone layer itself is being depleted by chronic environmental pollution, hence less UVB is being filtered from the atmosphere, and the incidence of skin cancer is proportionally on the rise. Since the same insult causes skin aging as causes skin cancer, skin aging too must be on the rise, though that increase is more difficult to quantify.

Exposure to the sun causes a whole range of reactions. Some are immediately detectable, and all are predictable. Response to sun exposure is familiar to all. An immediate reddening phase is followed by blistering and burning in some people and tanning in others. Gradual exposure affords protection from burning for many people, particularly darker individuals whose skin contains more melanin. This ability to tan varies from person to person and is ultimately dependent upon one's genetic origins. As a rule, fair-skinned northern Europeans tend to suffer sunburn while those of darker, southern ancestry tend to tan. The denser pigments of those of African descent provide the greatest protection of all. Since we are no longer separated by geography and few of us have descended in straight genetic lines, we must learn our own skin's reaction to the sun by trial and error. Nevertheless, these generalizations hold true.

Those with greater tanning ability are more tolerant of the sun, and the tan itself offers some measure of protection from the harmful effects of ultraviolet radiation. Sun-damaged skin, whether through tanning or burning, demonstrates characteristic changes under the microscope. They are primarily degenerative changes within the collagen layer of the dermis. These are the microscopic changes that result in loss of elasticity and wrinkling. The outer, epidermal layer becomes hyperactive, resulting in thickened surface irregularities and blotching of the skin. This coarse, loose, leathery, blotchy, wrinkled skin qualifies as prematurely aged. The changes seen under the microscope are specific, and can be clearly distinguished from the normal skin of an older individual. This extrinsic aging—that is, aging caused by external influences—superimposes coarse wrinkles, surface irregularities, abnormal blood vessels, loss of elasticity, and cancers on top of the fine wrinkling of normal aging. This is serious damage we are doing to ourselves. It is unnecessary and it is avoidable.

The worst of the damaging effects of the sun is increased susceptibility to skin cancer. According to the American Cancer Society, skin cancers currently develop at the rate of approximately a million lesions per year. Eighty percent of these are **basal cell carcinomas,** an easily treatable and easily curable lesion. Basal cell carcinomas arise from abnormal growth of the basal layer of the epidermis, hence the name. They were formerly called rodent ulcers for their frequent presentation as eroding ulcers of the skin, but the name did not present a true enough picture of the range of possible appearances of the lesion. It was also known as basal cell epithelioma. This was much less scary, because it implied the benign nature of the usual course of the lesion. But that name consequently seemed to encourage both physicians and the public to neglect the condition. So basal cell carcinoma it is. Technically a cancer, but one that behaves fairly benignly, it is easily cured. The lesions may take the form of persistent pimplelike eruptions, small ulcerations or sores that won't heal, shiny little skin bumps, and a number of other guises.

The key to treatment is early detection, and that requires alertness on both your part and that of your doctor. Basal cell carcinomas are often cured by the diagnostic biopsy alone, but don't count on it. They are slow-growing and very rarely metastasize. Death caused directly by this entity is virtually unheard of, but larger lesions can be deforming. Successful treatment depends on removing the entire lesion. This is accomplished by many means, including curettage (scraping), chemosurgery, and surgical removal. Surgical excision is a minor procedure done under local anesthetic in the doctor's office. It is the most favored method of treatment, because it produces a biopsy specimen from which the pathologist can quite accurately determine whether the lesion has been completely removed. Obviously, this is important, for if the lesion is incompletely removed it will continue to grow unless further excision is done. It is often difficult to determine the actual size of these lesions at the surface, as they often have an iceberg configuration, with more tumor beneath the surface than is visible to the eye. Complete removal is necessary for cure. Sometimes the problem is complicated by an odd location such as the tip of the nose or corner of the eye, but it should be curable; the size and area dictate the degree of resultant scarring. The objective is to find it early, cure it, and get on with life.

Basal cell carcinoma has long been known to be causally related to sun exposure. This effect is cumulative and manifested only years after damage. The basal cell carcinoma on the face of a fair-skinned forty-five-year-old usually reflects the sunburn and sun exposure of a lifetime. You cannot undo those years on the beach, baking to a golden brown, but you can stop doing additional damage and adding more risk now. Those most at risk are the fairest-skinned. Melanin, the protective pigment in the skin, determines susceptibility. It is found in least concentration in fair-skinned people, and that accounts for their increased risk. Melanin is the pigment that colors the skin. Darker skin means less likelihood of developing basal cell carcinoma from sun exposure. The darkest skin suffers the least risk of developing this problem. There are, however, exceptions, and there are numerous basal cell carcinomas found on body areas never exposed to the sun at all. Other factors are operative as well, but the most overwhelmingly powerful culprit is the sun. Fair-skinned people in sunny climates are the most likely targets, and the incidence decreases along the curve of skin pigment.

Most of the remaining 20 percent of skin cancers are **squamous cell carcinomas**. Approximately 160,000 new cases are reported yearly. This is a more dangerous disease. It is more difficult to eradicate and has a higher risk of spreading both locally and to distant sites. Therefore it must be dealt with more aggressively. The lesions usually look more like skin irritation or unhealed scabs and seem to grow rapidly. Treated early, they too are fairly easily curable. Squamous cell carcinomas are ultraviolet light related as well, and the distribution is again heavily weighted to the fair-skinned. Surgical excision is the treatment of choice, especially given the disease's ability to spread if not fully removed.

The third and last major type of skin cancer is **melanoma**. The American Cancer Society estimates 40,000 new cases yearly, and rising. This is very significant, for unless treated early, melanoma has deadly potential. The increase in incidence is thought to be related to increased exposure to ultraviolet rays. This represents new thinking, for a decade ago this link was essentially unknown. There is even talk that current sunblocks do not provide sufficient protection to reduce the risk of melanoma.

Melanoma is so named because it is an uncontrolled growth of the melanin-producing cells of the basal layer of the epidermis. These cells are called melanocytes, and they occur naturally in the skin in concentrations varying with skin type and situation. They are responsible for the pigmentation of the skin. An abnormal and uncontrolled growth of these cells in the early stages of the disease, before the cells break free and spread into the surrounding skin, is easily cured. Once the cells break free of their local restraints the lesion becomes dangerous. The treatment for melanoma is surgical, and it must be performed early in order to afford the best chance of cure.

Melanoma lesions typically present as dark spots on the skin, sometimes becoming darker, sometimes enlarging, and sometimes appearing like pigment spilling on the skin. Patients and physicians alike must be alert to the possibility of melanoma, and visual inspections are critical.

Here, too, one can see the importance of sun protection. Aging and wrinkling are an unpleasant reminder of the power of the sun, but the possibility of skin cancer makes a truly powerful case for protection.

Consider that 75 percent of an individual's ultraviolet exposure is accumulated before the age of twenty, yet skin cancer is a disease of middle age and older. Sun damage, like all radiation damage, is a cumulative phenomenon, and we pay for our transgressions long after those days at the beach. A recent Harvard Medical School study estimates that the use of effective sunblock during the first eighteen years of life would reduce the number of non-melanoma skin cancers by 78 percent. What this impressive number is telling us is that most sun exposure is in youth, and negative effects, which are seen much later, can actually be prevented by the use of sunblock. All this is absolutely clear. As evidence against unprotected sun exposure increases, we will become more diligent, but for most of us the damage has largely been done. What remains is to be vigilant for ourselves, avoid compounding the error, and protect the next generation from the mistakes made by ours. This will come to pass only when the positive value society places on suntan passes from our culture.

For the fair-skinned who plan to spend any time at all outdoors, sun protection must become a way of life, if only to reduce the risk of skin cancer.

We have already established that sun exposure is also the culprit in the premature aging of the skin. Here it runs a parallel course to its causative role in skin cancer. The facts are irrefutable. Sun exposure causes skin cancer and premature aging of the skin. Accept these facts and make the appropriate accommodations to manage them within your lifestyle. This is not meant to end the glories of outdoor living. There is little that you must deny yourself, nor must the slightest tan become a source of concern. That would be too extreme to be sensible. However, there is no longer any excuse to sunbathe unprotected. You must do what you can to minimize the damage while continuing to enjoy life.

If all this isn't enough, there is hard evidence that sun exposure depresses immune response. This is a general as well as local phenomenon, meaning that sun exposure in increasing amounts can cause generalized depression of the immune response as well as specific local events. An example of a specific local event is the reappearance of cold sores (herpes), particularly on the lips, on long, sunny vacations. Doesn't it seem strange that all that relaxation, baking in the sun, should result in an outbreak of herpes when you aren't being stressed at all? Obviously something more is going on, and that something is the reduced immune response that allows the permanently harbored but well-suppressed herpes to surface. It isn't clear whether this sort of anecdotal evidence combined with the measurable reduced immune response has any direct application to disease states, but there is food for thought at a time when the specter of immune disease is on the national conscience. Is there a relationship, even minute, between the suppression of sun exposure and the human response against HIV? The answer is unknown, but if we do not ask questions born of reasonable evidence, the answers will not be forthcoming. For now, it is merely an interesting thought, but further information is very likely around the corner.

Having said all this, the warm feeling of a day's activity in the sun is regenerating indeed, and you can enjoy it without doing harm. A wide-brimmed hat, sunscreen, and common sense are all you need to do so.

Sunblocks and Sunscreens

Of the various means of sun protection, sunblocks and sunscreens are the most recent to become part of our lives. Their use is not simple avoidance or cover-up, but rather scientific in its workings, replete with choices and claims, and thoroughly confusing.

Sunscreens fall into one of two categories, physical and chemical. The physical sunscreens are very close to being sunblocks, because they work as physical barriers, preventing the sun from reaching the skin. Zinc oxide, the thick white stuff that lifeguards put on their noses, is an example. These compounds are effective at reflecting the light from the skin, thereby protecting the skin from damage, and can properly be called sunblocks. Other frequently used barriers include titanium dioxide, iron oxide, magnesium silicate, and other opaque, reflective materials. The downside of these compounds is that they have long been difficult to apply in a pleasant and invisible coat. But they work, and work well. Some of these blocking agents, such as titanium dioxide, are now being produced in a relatively clear preparation, which has been added to sunscreen to achieve the fullest range of protection.

Far more popular are the chemical sunscreens. These compounds work as filters, absorbing the ultraviolet spectrum. Most people prefer these over sunblocks because of their ease of application and the gradual and limited tanning they allow. Best known among this group is para-aminobenzoic acid (PABA). This is a very effective compound, but it has fallen from favor because of the high incidence of allergy and skin irritation associated with its use. Other related compounds have taken up the slack. Frequently used active ingredients include oxybenzone, dioxybenzone, salicylates, cinnamates, and anthranilates.

These ingredients, and others, are quite effective. You will find one or more of them listed among the ingredients of whatever sunscreen you currently use. In addition to the list of ingredients, the package will be clearly marked with the sun protection factor (SPF) of the product. The SPF is based on the laboratory-determined time required for sunscreen-protected skin to exhibit a particular level of sunburn compared with the time required for the same level of sunburn on unprotected skin. If your skin would burn in half an hour unprotected, the use of a product with an SPF of 2 would allow an hour in the sun before burning—double the exposure before the same level of sunburn was reached. Therefore the very popular SPF 15 products should allow the same individual fifteen times the unprotected exposure time. But does a single application of SPF 15 sunscreen really afford seven and a half hours of protection? I doubt it. These calculations are based on laboratory data, not real life. They cannot take into account the actual conditions of the moment, whether the sunscreen was applied evenly and thickly enough, whether it was sweated off or washed away in the water, or the actual propensity to burn of each individual under varying circumstances. The SPF of a product is merely a guide. SPF 15 will do more to protect you than SPF 6, but it too must be reapplied regularly over the course of a day's exposure. There is little possible harm in too much protection, and if you use the same product repeatedly you will soon learn how frequently it must be applied for your individual circumstances. There is no substitute for intelligent observation and self-help.

Sunscreens are available with SPF ratings of 30, 45, and 50. Are these a great advance in protection? Maybe not. The standard for adequate protection is SPF 15, which filters out some 92–93 percent of the sun's rays. The higher SPF ratings filter perhaps another 4–5 percent of the sunlight. Is that enough to get excited about? Most experts think it isn't. In fact, the FDA believes a limit of SPF 30 should be imposed. This would do much to avoid confusion. What is more disturbing than a little marketing hype is the dangerous false sense of security these high-SPF products engender. They are most frequently used on first exposure for the season or tropical vacation, when protection is critical. And fair-skinned individuals have also adopted them for general protection. Certainly these products are every bit as good as SPF 15 sunscreens, and even filter out an additional 2 or 3 percent, but they too must be reapplied regularly, and that's the problem—they give one a false sense of security. The best bet is repeated application of the SPF 15 product you are accustomed to using. Laboratory values and actual practice are rarely the same, and a little healthy caution goes a long way.

Some of the active ingredients in sunscreens are absorbed into the keratinized external layer of the skin. Therefore, residual protection from yesterday's application is carried over to today. But there is no evidence at all that this offers anything like full protection. It is always a good idea to reapply before going out in the sun. Fair individuals should use sunscreen for even the casual exposure of daily life. Those living in warmer climates or high altitudes should follow the same precautions. The danger from casual exposure to the sun in Miami or reflected rays at high altitude on slopes at Aspen far exceeds that of a Chicago winter.

For active periods, there are water-resistant and waterproof sunscreens available. These products are very useful, but again a note of caution should be injected. Waterproof sunscreens are not perfect, and need regular reapplication.

Water-resistant means that the product continues to protect after forty minutes of immersion. **Waterproof** means it protects for up to eighty minutes of immersion.

For the most part, these products are easy to use, but they are typically not as easy or pleasant to use as the well-formulated general-use sunscreens. For a day at the beach they are certainly worth a try.

Tan Enhancers and Self-tanning Lotions

Other products that cause a bit of confusion are various forms of tan enhancers and self-tanning compounds. Some tan enhancers are in disfavor with the FDA either because they rely on enzymatic action, which has not proved effective, or, as is the case with some European products, they have caused cancer in laboratory animals. Most are conceptually dangerous unless they contain sunscreens in significant concentration to offer protection as well. Usually they do not, since sunscreen would do little to enhance suntan. Any product that helps produce a natural tan is exposing the user to the risks of ultraviolet radiation—not very different from the suntan oil of the old days. It is also important not to overestimate the protective value of an established tan against future exposure. Even when these products contain small amounts of sunscreen they are barely more effective than no sunscreen at all. If you use nothing at all, at least you won't be fooling yourself.

Self-tanning lotions and gels are different from tan enhancers. They are based on the active ingredient dihydroxyacetone (DHA), which dyes the skin. It has been used for decades and seems safe. The newer products produce a relatively natural-looking tan, not the sickly orange cast associated with the previous generation of sun-free tanners. A concentration of 3 to 5 percent DHA seems most popular. The color lasts several days and has the downside of staining the nails and hair if not neatly applied or washed off immediately after use.

These self-tanning products produce dyed skin, not melanin coloration, and therefore offer no "natural" protection from the sun unless a sunscreen is included in the formulation, or applied separately. If you feel you need a tan, and the color suits you, this may be an alternative to damaging your skin in the sun.

Sunglasses

Another form of sun protection of increasingly well-documented importance is sunglasses. Long favored for fashion and comfort, sunglasses are also important for the preservation of vision. First, and most important, it is clear that exposure to sunlight hastens the formation of cataracts. These opaque changes in the lens of the eye gradually impede vision and must be treated surgically. A direct relationship has been established between the onset of cataracts and unprotected exposure to ultraviolet radiation.

Most sunglasses are treated to filter out ultraviolet radiation, particularly the destructive UVB band. There have been repeatedly demonstrated correlations between UV exposure and early cataract development, some quite dramatic. An interesting 1994 paper analyzed Medicare data on some one million surgical cataract extractions for any number of variable causes, concluding that the strongest indicator of likelihood of cataract surgery is the latitude of a person's residence. This closely relates to the amount of UVB in sunlight. The penetration of radiation differs at each angle of incidence of the sun to earth, the angle being more direct the closer one gets to the equator. In fact, the data in the continental United States show a 3 percent increased likelihood of cataract formation with each degree of movement south. Small wonder ophthalmologists have followed the cardiologists to Florida.

A side benefit of sunglasses use is less squinting and frowning to reduce the light, and thus fewer wrinkles formed around the eyes and between the eyebrows where the muscles of facial expression are folding the skin.

ANTIOXIDANT THERAPY

Any serious discussion of **free radicals** and **antioxidants** could not have taken place ten years ago. Though little of the science itself is actually new, its application to human health in general and antiaging in particular is very recent. At the most basic level, free radicals are negatively charged oxygen particles, producing what is essentially a free electron, which enters into destructive chemical reactions with substances such as proteins. This results in oxidation, or a sort of chemical burning of the substance, which denatures or destroys it. Proteins such as collagen are denatured and genes are broken, and potentially dangerous residual substances may result from the chemical reaction.

The naturally occurring compounds known to neutralize these destructive reactions are called antioxidants, and we have known about them for a long time. The most familiar forms are vitamins, both naturally occurring and in supplements. While there was never any doubt about the value of fruit and vegetables in the diet, the mode of action and actual worth of supplemental vitamins was questioned by the experts even as food and health faddists adopted their use and claimed all manner of miracles. Well-designed laboratory studies and large-scale clinical trials conducted over years have proved the use of antioxidants effective on many fronts.

Any number of the activities of daily living have been shown to increase the presence of negatively charged oxygen free radicals in the body. Exposure to sunlight is known to lead to oxidative destruction of the skin associated with an increased incidence of skin cancer and the breakdown of collagen and elastin, causing laxity of the skin and wrinkles. If you know something of the action of ultraviolet radiation, that may not come as a surprise. However, strenuous aerobic exercise, which we all believe to be the road to eternal life, is also associated with increased circulating free radicals and tissue damage. The production of free radicals is a function of normal metabolism, which is usually neutralized by antioxidant enzymes and diet-derived antioxidants. This group includes vitamin E, vitamin C (ascorbic acid), and carotenes, among others.

The chemical name of **vitamin E** is alpha-tocopherol. It is the major nonenzymatic antioxidant protecting the skin from the adverse effects of sun damage and aging. It has been shown to reverse several elements of the damage caused by the sun and actually stimulates new collagen formation.

Antioxidants are thought to be instrumental in reversing the oxidation and calcification of cholesterol, the precursor to atherosclerosis and potential blockage of the coronary arteries. And as their effects are uncovered, increasingly far-reaching aspects are sought, with interesting and often surprising results—not all of them pleasant. Two well-constructed studies of the effect of the potent antioxidant beta-carotene were reported over the last year. They were carried out in the United States and Finland using large populations of smokers, and attempted to find salutary effects of beta-carotene usage against the onset of lung cancer in this statistically at-risk group. Naturally, the thinking was that this drug, so successful in the prevention of heart disease, could apply its antioxidant magic and cell-repairing powers against cancer. The findings, to everyone's dismay, indicated a higher risk of lung cancer among the beta-carotene users than nonusers. Both studies yielded similar results and caused the government to advise men to discontinue the use of beta-carotene as part of their anticoronary strategy. So, things aren't always what we expect them to be, and these findings remain unexplained.

Such has not been the case with vitamin E, which has thus far been free of any important negative implications. If all this seems capricious and unscientific, one must factor in the manner in which all this information is accumulated. Most of what we know is derived from statistical analyses of various human groups divided into substance users and substance nonusers. The results are measured in serum blood levels, symptoms, longevity, or whatever parameters are being studied. These studies are usually conducted over many years, from initial interest in the subject, to devising the study, to the ultimate result. Studies become almost absurdly long when measuring human longevity, which of course is the ultimate test. The Framingham study, upon which so much of our coronary disease information is based, has been tracked for nearly fifty years. In properly constructed studies of large numbers of individuals in which the insidious effect of external forces upon longevity is measured, there is a long wait between concept and interpretation of results, often decades. Additionally, there is always great difficulty separating other possibly influential factors, or variables, from the issue being studied. Taken together, and in the face of ethical considerations, human health studies are difficult to perform, difficult to evaluate, and often subject to reevaluation and change.

After that precaution, let's consider the positive side of vitamin E. It has been found effective in limiting the oxidation of low-density and very-low-density lipoproteins and their conversion into cholesterol plaques. It appears to be important in the repair of the intimal lining of blood vessels, and it is known to have a markedly positive effect on skin. All this with no appreciable downside. Much of this information on the coronary-sparing nature of vitamin E has surfaced recently.

Other vitamins studied in the same manner, with startlingly impressive results, include folic acid and vitamin B_6. These have been found to reduce the incidence of heart attack by more than 30 percent in a study group of nurses through middle age. There is every reason to project equally impressive statistics for men, according to comments by experts when results of the study were made public in early 1998. The study also reiterated findings of decreased coronary risk with moderate daily alcohol intake. The proposed method of operation of vitamin B_6 and folic acid is in the promotion of the HDL (high-density lipoprotein) cholesterol content of the blood ("good" cholesterol) and secondary reduction of levels of the amino acid homocysteine. All this is good news, and one should incorporate vitamin B_6, folic acid, vitamin E, and vitamin C supplements in the daily routine.

Exactly how much vitamin E is necessary for optimal antioxidant functions is unknown, and so is the most effective method to deliver it to the skin or the organ in question. Dietary intake of foods rich in antioxidants and intake of vitamin E supplements both increase the measurable serum levels and therefore remain the routes of choice. There is no scientific evidence that rubbing vitamin E onto the skin does any good at all. The molecule is too large to penetrate the skin, and should not work. There are those who swear by this direct skin application therapy, but their evidence is decidedly less than scientific and only serves to confuse the issue. When and if an effective method of delivering vitamin E directly to the skin, bypassing digestion and absorption, is developed, it will be of great importance.

So how much vitamin E should you take? Current dietary advice from most official sources indicates that a diet rich in fruits and vegetables should provide adequate vitamin E for normal, healthy adults. But it is hard to accept this advice when so little about the beneficial effects was known until recently, and various official sources, both governmental and medical, move excruciatingly slowly in acknowledging change. There is also no evidence that 400 to 1,000 international units of vitamin E supplement taken daily does any harm at all, and every indication that it does considerable good. Therefore it seems prudent to suggest this dosage as a daily supplement of vitamin E.

Along with vitamin E, the most popular antioxidant supplement is **vitamin C,** ascorbic acid. There is evidence that when used in combination, vitamin E and vitamin C exhibit greater antioxidant effect than either alone, but no hard numbers are available. For our purposes, it is best to consider these two potent antioxidants separately, but use them together.

In recent years vitamin C has been given credit for all sorts of miracles, proven and unproven. It is well known for its role in wound healing and maintaining tissue integrity through its pivotal function in collagen synthesis. Understanding of vitamin C unfolded gradually over more than two centuries, with the pace picking up in the last decade or so.

Vitamin C became of historical significance when its absence caused the disease scurvy among British sailors long at sea. The disease resulted in tissue breakdown and open sores, which could be prevented by inclusion in the diet of fresh citrus fruit, usually in the form of limes, now known to be high in stored vitamin C. Limes became staples on long voyages, hence the term *limey* for British sailors.

Linus Pauling, famous as the winner of both the Nobel Prize for chemistry in 1954 and the Nobel Peace Prize in 1962, became obsessed with vitamin C in 1966. His involvement meant instant recognition for the compound and was the start of a fadlike movement that may have driven serious scientists away even as the lay public joined it. Pauling advocated daily doses of 6,000 to 18,000 milligrams of vitamin C. This massive intake was said to cure virtually everything and to hold heart disease and cancer at bay. There was some evidence of the beneficial effect of antioxidants, and some of the lifestyle modifications he espoused have held true. Still, most of this evidence was circumstantial at best. Over the years it became apparent that massive doses were excreted, and might actually have negative effects. Claims of intestinal cancer in laboratory animals subjected to proportionally high doses appeared in the literature, and a scientific backlash developed.

Many of Pauling's claims have not been borne out, but he did provide the impetus for much of the serious research done over the last two decades. Among the promised effects was the ability of vitamin C to help ward off various diseases, most notably the common cold. This provided a famous battleground between the forces of science and the popular health culture. Many individuals, physicians included, believed they became ill less frequently and less severely with the use of vitamin C, but there was no firm scientific basis for this claim. A study testing the hypothesis was constructed by Dr. Thomas Chalmers, at the Mount Sinai Medical Center in New York, and published in 1975.

Initial results of the Chalmers study showed no positive effects of vitamin C usage on the severity and duration of the common cold, and for a short while it seemed to fall from favor. However, soon thereafter another group challenged the findings by measuring the responses of patients taking significantly higher doses of vitamin C at the first sign of cold symptoms. Both the duration and the severity of the symptoms were significantly reduced in the group taking vitamin C compared with the controls. This was the first time the medical establishment had license to encourage the use of antioxidants, and soon thereafter the floodgates opened. Over the last ten years, vitamin C has become well entrenched in the popular vocabulary of preventive medicine.

The role of vitamin C in collagen production was an important finding, providing a pivotal insight into the biology of wound healing and tissue building. As a very potent antioxidant, vitamin C helps maintain the integrity of the skin in the face of aging. Acting as it does to prevent the oxidation of cholesterol, it appears important in protecting the coronary arteries from the production of calcified plaques of cholesterol. Vitamin C also impedes the formation of cataracts and may be important in the prevention of macular degeneration. It is generally acknowledged to be important in an increasing number of roles. But the level necessary for it to fulfill these roles remains unclear.

Despite evidence to the contrary, dietary vitamin C, as provided by citrus fruits and vegetables, has long been deemed sufficient to meet bodily needs. Most proponents suggest daily supplements in the range of 1,000 milligrams, though this recommendation too is unsupported by hard facts. In 1966 a study supported by the National Institutes of Health found no apparent value in doses of vitamin C exceeding 400 milligrams. This was based on measured saturation of the white blood cells and plasma at this level and the inability of the body to absorb additional amounts. The study also conceded that amounts above 1,000 milligrams per day may promote kidney stones in susceptible individuals.

Based on the available research, I recommend a daily supplement of 1,000 milligrams of vitamin C. This seems an appropriate maintenance level at which one would benefit from the effects of this potent antioxidant without entering uncharted territory.

There is currently much interest in the effects of vitamin C applied to the skin. This stems from animal studies showing decreased redness from sun exposure when vitamin

C is applied either before or after exposure. There is also speculation, based on early evidence, that topical vitamin C may prevent local immune suppression caused by ultraviolet radiation. This is all in the presumptive stages, but vitamin C topical products are promising everything. It remains to be seen what concentration of vitamin C is necessary to protect the skin or aid in collagen production and repair, and how to deliver these amounts through the skin.

Another antioxidant that has assumed mythical powers is **beta-carotene**, but it has fallen dramatically from grace, as I have already mentioned. Closely related to vitamin A and thought to be effective both in the prevention of cancer and the oxidation of cholesterol, this supplement was all the rage in the early 1990s. In 1996 a study was published in the *Journal of the National Cancer Institute* reporting an increased lung cancer rate among smokers taking beta-carotene supplements compared with those not receiving the supplements. Though complicated by numerous variables, this study was conducted on a large scale and at very least points to the need for more research into the effects of beta-carotene. Other recent studies have indicated little effect of beta-carotene in the prevention of heart disease. The evidence suggests the abandonment of beta-carotene until further notice.

A final point about the antioxidants concerns the natural form of the various compounds. Much of the evidence that they protect against cancer and heart disease has been culled from comparative studies of those consuming diets rich in vitamins in their natural state—diets heavily weighted with fruits and vegetables, which are the natural source of antioxidants. Such eating habits are usually practiced by those whose lifestyle is generally healthy. Hence, it becomes difficult to pinpoint positive influences. Once a health idea catches on, it is difficult to persuade the faithful to abandon it for the good of science. After all, we only go around once, and each of us wants the best shot. The "purified" pulverized and capsulated vitamins we are so familiar with are thought to have the beneficial effects of the natural sources they are meant to emulate. This is generally the case, though there is an extra element in the real thing that cannot be identified or emulated. All else being equal, it is prudent to consume a healthy diet, rich in fruit and vegetables and low in fat, rather than rely solely on vitamin supplements. By all means take the supplements. Study after study shows that they work. But don't abandon the real thing—it may work better.

DIET AND WEIGHT CONTROL

As we have seen repeatedly, concern for one's appearance cannot be isolated from concern for overall good health. Appearance and health go hand in hand. Diet and exercise are critical parts of the equation. Without a healthy diet, stable weight, and reasonable regular exercise it is impossible to look and feel one's best. Sure, there are the genetically endowed among us who can eat like pigs, live sedentary lives, and still look great, but they are the exception. And in fact, even the lucky few would do significantly better in many ways if they weren't fighting their bodies at every turn.

Among the most basic human goals are good health and longevity. These are natural consequences of genetic inheritance and proper life habits, and each exerts a powerful influence on one's potential. We are often able to modify the course of events written in our genes by lifestyle alterations. This change can be for better or worse, as the outcome is truly some balance between inborn tendencies and behavior. A most glaring example of this is the influence of diet and exercise upon general health. Proper diet and exercise are critical to health and longevity, and must be considered. If you can't internalize these simple concepts, you are probably wasting your time worrying about the details of looking good.

Weight gain is unhealthy on the most basic level. It taxes the heart beyond normal capacity and is associated with hyperlipemia (excess lipids in the blood) and cholesterol deposits in the coronary arteries. As a side effect, it stretches the skin out of shape. Beyond early adulthood, one cannot expect the skin to expand and contract with swings in weight. The elastic component of the skin responsible for a proper fit cannot survive this sort of abuse, and after a point it will simply fail to conform. Small weight variations of 2 percent of body weight are perceptible but not significant, as the body accommodates easily to the change. Infrequent weight changes of up to 5 percent of body weight are well tolerated. This would be 7¾ pounds for a 155-pound man. Sometimes the skin can accommodate a 10 percent loss—15½ pounds for a 155-pound man—without obvious laxity. This becomes increasingly unlikely as middle age nears, and virtually impossible thereafter. Obviously the strategy is weight maintenance.

More than half the male population in the United States carries 10 percent above their suggested optimal weight. Virtually all of these individuals have lost significant weight more than once and subsequently regained it. The old joke about the man who tells amazed listeners he lost 300 pounds—10 pounds thirty times—is not far from the truth. Weight loss is the product of inspiration. Keeping the weight off is boring, hard work. It requires re-education and change from the lifestyle that allowed weight gain.

The 70-kilogram (155-pound) man needs approximately 2,000 calories daily. You may not weigh 155 pounds, but most studies use this point of reference. Typically, calculations are based on the 70-kilogram man. At 2.2 pounds per kilogram, 70 kilograms is about 155 pounds, and adopting this standard means that all researchers are using the same model. This caloric input will sustain basic bodily functions as well as the normal sedentary lifestyle.

The calorie content of a New York bagel hovers at just over 300 calories—without cream cheese, butter, or other fillers. A Snickers bar weighs in at 280 calories, and a Big Mac, fries, and a Coke total 1,160. That nearly covers the day's needs. Add cream cheese to the bagel and that results in weight gain.

How about the calories needed to sustain work, exercise, and the extraordinary bodily functions of daily life? The sad news is that running a mile in ten minutes expends only 145 calories. An hour of tennis singles or fast walking consumes less than 250 calories. And an hour of sex? Sadly, only 150 calories, immediately neutralized by a Coke at 160 calories. In other words, exercise is not the road to weight loss, restricted caloric intake is.

It is virtually impossible for the average person to consume enough energy through exercise alone to effect quantifiable, sustained weight loss. Forget about the legendary five-pound weight loss reported by baseball pitchers on hot August afternoons. That represents water loss and is soon replaced. You can't work it off. Restricted intake is the only solution.

There are a number of retraining routines to get you started along the proper road, but it is imperative to fully internalize the importance of the project to make it palatable. Simply looking better should be enough motivation, but there is more. Feeling good and feeling proud are important rewards, but longevity and good health are the most important benefits of proper diet and nutrition, and they are inextricably intertwined. The relationship between dietary saturated fat and heart disease remains complicated by factors such as the individual's own cholesterol production and the genetic tendency toward heart disease. Nevertheless, men who exercise, follow fat-restricted diets, refrain from smoking, and are not overweight are significantly less likely to die of coronary artery disease than had they not met those criteria. The effect of weight and diet cannot be overestimated. It is generally agreed that calorie restriction is the route to longevity. Numerous studies in small animals and primates have demonstrated 30 to 50 percent increased life span with calorie restriction. There is every reason to believe the same relationship holds true for humans, though the length of our life span precludes controlled studies. Few have volunteered to submit to decades of constant hunger for the good of science. Still, there is evidence that calorie restriction is the right track.

There are so many nearly proven theories linking diet and weight to coronary artery disease that it becomes difficult to ignore. I continue to advise a fad-free (not fat-free), low-fat diet of restricted volume, which translates to fewer calories. No fad diet ever works, though each and every one will provide initial weight loss. Unfortunately, this is a setup for yo-yo weight gain and loss, because you have not retrained yourself. The quick-fix diet is impossible to stick with and, over the long haul, is unhealthy. If you eat eight grapefruits a day and nothing else, you will lose weight. If you allow yourself unlimited steak, and steak alone, you will quickly become revolted by the thought of it, eat less, and lose weight. Low protein, high protein, low carbohydrate, all carbohydrate, no carbohydrate . . . whatever. None of these is a code to live by, and as soon as one tires of the diet, the weight returns. You have learned nothing and gained nothing—nothing but the weight you worked so hard to shed. Though this topic alone could fill a book, here are five simple rules for weight maintenance that are sure to help.

1. **Begin each meal with a full glass of water.** This is an effective expedient to slake hunger.
2. **Leave some of every portion on your plate.**
3. **Never have seconds!**
4. **No desserts.**
5. **Fresh fruit is the only acceptable between-meal snack.** It satisfies hunger, is digested slowly, and releases sugars over an extended period.

These simple rules are invaluable as a first step to retraining one's approach to food. They do not constitute a diet, and will not do much toward weight loss, but they are the basis for lifelong maintenance. Once they become part of your routine it will be easy to use whatever method you choose for quick weight loss and hold on to the progress you make. The idea of controlling your caloric intake becomes easier once you have done it. One is soon cognizant of the adjustments necessary for loss and maintenance.

When one considers diet and nutrition, a world of half-truths surfaces from every magazine rack and bookshelf. That there are so many opinions, both unsupported and unrefuted, should make clear how very little we know. Moderation and common sense are the rule, and while there are no absolutes, a few valid guidelines do exist.

Restrict intake of saturated fat. This is strictly a cardiac strategy, and though it is not as crucial for some men as for others, heart attack remains the leading cause of death among men, and saturated fat is one of the culprits. Red meat and dairy products are sources of most dietary saturated fat, but snack foods are full of fat too and do their share of the damage. Chose your indulgences carefully, and discuss the situation with your doctor.

Substitute monounsaturated fats. These include primarily olive oil and canola oil. Monounsaturated fats seem unrelated to the oxidation and calcification of cholesterol and may even help reverse the process. They also raise the "good" cholesterol, the HDL fraction, and therefore should be healthy.

Remember that fat, any kind of fat, represents nine calories per gram of intake, compared with four calories per gram for protein or carbohydrate. Reduce fat consumption, if only for weight control.

Find a routine that is comfortable for you, and stick to it. For the last twenty years I have had nothing more for breakfast than orange juice, vitamin C, vitamin E, and coffee. I have water, fruit, or fat-free snacks on operating days, a rare lunch otherwise, and anything I desire for dinner. With time this has come to mean less and less red meat and more pasta and vegetables. With trial and error I have found this formula effective in keeping my weight stable within a window of two or three pounds. It will work for you as well. Experiment and find your own balance.

EXERCISE

To hear all the talk, exercise is the panacea for modern society. It is important for many reasons, but I do not mean to endorse the cult that has grown around the daily workout, run, and swim. Exercise should be a part of your life, not the central focus. There may be perils associated with too much exercise, which is of no interest to the present discussion. What is pertinent is the amount and type of exercise necessary to keep you looking your best for the longest time. For the most part, health benefits and appearance follow a parallel course, and we will not lose sight of that aspect of the workout.

Exercise is classified as aerobic or anaerobic, depending on the metabolic pathway fueling the muscles. Aerobic exercise became part of our lives in the form of ridiculous television exercise programs and best-selling videos and books. For the most part the appeal was to women, who promptly became fit enough to live forever. The most enthusiastic converts were women under fifty, who adopted regular exercise with religious zeal. Unfortunately this is the group least in need of aerobically increasing their cardiovascular reserve. This group of premenopausal women are in the lowest risk group for coronary disease, far better off than men of the same age, men over fifty, and menopausal women. Older women, beyond fifty, and usually postmenopausal, lose the coronary-sparing effect of natural estrogen, and if they don't begin estrogen substitution therapy, are nearly as likely as men of the same age to suffer heart attack. Men, for the most part, bypassed the aerobic routines in favor of running, which is based on the same premise.

There is reasonably good evidence that aerobic exercise increases one's chances of survival after a heart attack. This is predicated on the increased ability of the heart muscle to thrive under conditions of diminished oxygen availability. The exercise serves to simulate these conditions by holding the heart rate at near-maximal rate for protracted periods of time. The cardiovascular benefits of running are similarly derived, as are exercises like stair climbing, rowing, and bicycling. Running is far and away the most popular option, and from my point of view, that is unfortunate. Given that running does the job, is reasonably pleasant, social, and socially acceptable, and is easy to feel part of, one can understand the devotion it engenders. There is also the side benefit of the residual elevation of metabolism after distance running, which, combined with ketosis and high levels of circulating free radicals, burns calories and decreases appetite, resulting in weight loss, or, more likely, weight control.

Unfortunately, that weight loss, when there is any, begins in the subcutaneous fat of the face, resulting in the gaunt look of long-distance runners. The constant pounding of heel to road, forward spring, and heel to road again creates a whiplash movement of the soft tissue of the face. The cheeks rise and crash down with each step, pulling on their attachment to underlying structures and stretching the elastic fibers. This motion is readily captured in slow-motion pictures of the face of a running man. The same principle applies to women. I often point out that they wouldn't dare run without a running bra to protect the breasts from this very same movement. Yet the very visible cheeks are allowed to pull and stretch, accelerating the loss of elasticity and aging.

Then there is the damage to the articular cartilage of the knees and ankles from the constant pounding, and the traumatic arthritis that results. There is also a substantial incidence of cardiac problems among unfit runners.

Recent studies indicate that fast walking for twenty minutes daily has the same positive cardiovascular effect and is far less traumatic to the joints and skin. There are no reported deaths from fast walking, either because the heart rate is raised less rapidly during this mild exercise or for other unexplained reasons. In any event, it works. Rowing, stair climbing, and particularly bicycling, which can be experienced as a pleasant outdoor event, provide the same benefits.

Anaerobic exercise describes muscle work requiring more energy than the available oxygen supply can produce. Alternative metabolic pathways become necessary to fuel this heavy muscle work. This is the case in weight training and heavy labor. In this way weight training differs from aerobics, which utilizes available oxygen. Anaerobic exercise increases muscle strength and lean muscle mass, but it has little cardiovascular value. This is the exercise that makes you look better but not live longer.

"Muscle building" is a confusing phrase. It conjures visions of greased bodies flexing chiseled biceps, but it need not be that at all. It is the rare individual who can maintain his anatomical potential without actual physical work, whether at labor or in the gym. Good muscle tone encourages good posture, bearing, and self-image. In the active years it provides strength and stamina for physical activities, and is a major element in preventing sports injuries. In later years exercise maintains muscle mass, which in turn increases bone density, preventing osteoporosis and fractures. Recent studies of sedentary individuals in their seventies and eighties have shown marked increases in bone density in response to weight training. A study published in *The New England Journal of Medicine* reports muscle fiber regeneration in nonagenarians on a weight-training regime. These elderly individuals also performed significantly better in tasks such as stair climbing, speed walking, and actual lifting. Reversing muscle loss and increasing bone density represent major markers in the quest to reverse aging. These had previously been considered quantifiable and reliable signs of old age.

What does all this mean? Clearly, aerobic exercise alone is not sufficient. Muscles are meant to work against resistance, and to maintain proper condition they must work. Since most of us do little physical labor, we must find a substitute, and as we have recently learned, this should be a lifelong routine, one that will yield demonstrable and desirable returns.

Most experts encourage an hour of combined aerobic and anaerobic training every other day. There seem to be cumulative benefits of combined workout, making it preferable to avoid separation of aerobic and anaerobic phases. During the most active decades of life, many men cannot adhere to a routine, and they work out less frequently than they should. Some unscientific soft evidence shows diminishing benefits with fewer than three sessions weekly. Exercise physiologists encourage a day of rest between exercise of specific muscle groups, so those who feel a void without a daily workout are encouraged to rotate areas. Aerobic workouts may be repeated at will.

At some point one runs the risk of crossing an imaginary line between utilizing the function of exercise for a healthier, longer, and more functional life and exercise as an end in itself. Though most of us eschew competitive bodybuilding as an example of a good thing taken unproductively far, we were willing to accept marathon running as reasonable. In recent years the tables have turned. Bulging biceps and a flat abdomen are sought after, and the destructive pounding of marathon training, if not totally yielding to more sensible routines, has become simply a goal to reach instead of a lifelong routine. The proper mix of exercise routines changes with the style of the time, influenced, for the sensible, by knowledge. Moderation and common sense will help exercise work for you. If running feels good, do it—but in moderation. Substitute low-impact aerobics for half your workouts, and your knees will thank you. Huge, sculpted muscles may appeal to some, but keeping them from turning to fat at sixty is difficult. Aerobics and weight training are part of the route to a longer, healthier life. It takes work, and it takes common sense. Make it work for you, not against you.

The exercise regime I recommend incorporates the elements necessary for cardiovascular fitness and good muscle tone, and it is applicable to all active, healthy adult men. Younger men training for athletic pursuits will need different, more specific routines, as will older men and men with infirmities. This program will achieve visible results in virtually every man within six weeks. Those results may be measured in increased cardiovascular performance, muscle strength, and endurance, and if you are not too fat for it to show, better muscle tone.

The program is called **10/15/20,** for reasons that will soon be clear. It was devised with the help of exercise counselor Joan Pagano, a popular and respected training specialist in New York. The idea is to make the program so simple and transportable that there is no excuse not to keep on track. It will take no more than one hour daily, and is designed to be performed every other day. Three times a week works fine. Twice a week is the bare minimum. Less than that loses momentum and is self-defeating.

Aerobic, cardiovascular exercise can take many forms. It requires full bodywork at a pace that is quite tolerable, but elevates heart rate significantly. Running, which I am not in favor of for reasons I've made apparent, is the most common of these. Bicycling, stationary bike riding, rowing, stair climbing, rope skipping, and fast walking do the job every bit as well and reduce the wear and tear on the joints, back, and soft tissue that comes with running. These should be done at least three times weekly for twenty minutes per session. Such exercise won't make you live forever, but it will help you live longer.

Weight training is imperative to preserve muscle mass, posture, and strength. It also makes you look good. This too is an every-other-day routine. I have included eight exercises, which cover most of the major muscle groups. These are performed initially with fifteen-pound dumbbells. These are inexpensive, can be stored anywhere, and don't require membership in a gym, although that is not a bad idea. The exercises are done as two sets of ten repetitions, increasing to fifteen repetitions as strength and endurance grow, then changing to twenty-pound weights for various exercises. This will happen quickly. Increasing reps and weights vary from man to man, and it is a good policy to have periodic sessions with a trainer to evaluate progress and alter routines when necessary. Without the luxury of a trainer, common sense must be one's guide. Don't do what you cannot, and don't struggle. There is nothing to be gained but the risk of injuring yourself. Start slowly and sensibly. Older men and those who haven't exercised in years should start with lighter weights and fewer repetitions.

The name "10/15/20" refers to the number of exercises in the routine, the initial weight used, and the time spent at aerobics. Ten exercises are performed, using fifteen-pound free weights, after twenty minutes of aerobics. The program will suit the majority of men, though you may be the exception. If so, find the combination that suits you, and do it.

The 10/15/20 Exercise Routine

1. **Aerobic workout**. Start slowly as a warm-up, and build to twenty minutes of any of the aerobic exercises that appeal to you. More than twenty minutes is not necessary for standard cardiovascular fitness. You must check your pulse rate periodically to achieve the necessary work level. This should approximate 120 beats per minute at work, though the training zone varies widely, depending on one's resting heart rate. Then rest and stretch before beginning weight training.

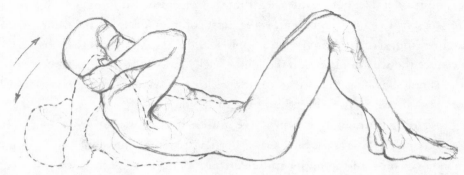

Abdominal crunch

2. Abdominal crunches to strengthen and tone the rectus abdominus muscles (abs). This simple partial sit-up, done without weights, is performed on the back with knees bent and hands behind the head. The head and shoulders are elevated from the horizontal to a thirty-degree position, then lowered. This is repeated twenty times initially, then increased as strength builds. Crunches are easier to perform and less potentially damaging than sit-ups for the average man.

Pullover, using individual weights

3. Pullovers for shoulder and back muscles. Performed on floor with knees flexed. A fifteen-pound dumbbell is held at the ends and with arms bent is brought from shoulders extended over head to over chest position. Individually held free weights are used as fitness develops. Two sets of fifteen repetitions are performed.

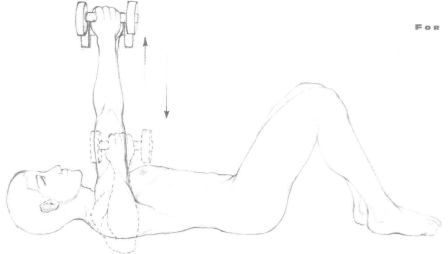

Fly

4. Flies for shoulder and pectoralis muscles. Done on the floor or flat bench with knees bent and a fifteen-pound weight in each hand. The weights traverse from outstretches at shoulder height to meet over the chest. Arms are flexed at ninety degrees throughout. Two sets of fifteen repetitions.

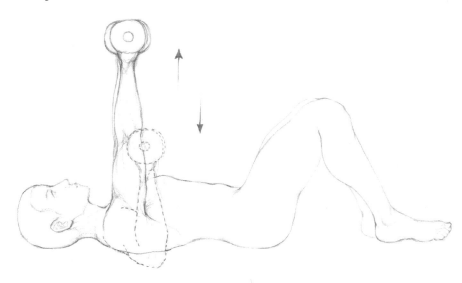

Flat press

5. Flat presses from the same flat position as above, with knees bent. This exercise is for the anterior shoulder and chest, and is done at shoulder height by fully extending the arms. Two sets of fifteen repetitions.

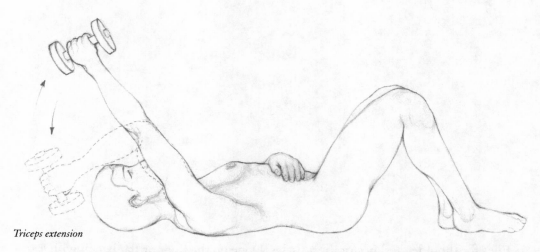

Triceps extension

6. Triceps extensions from the same position, either one- or two-handed, for the triceps muscle at the back of the upper arm. Arm carrying weight is extended. This can be done flat or standing, whichever is more comfortable. Two sets of fifteen reps.

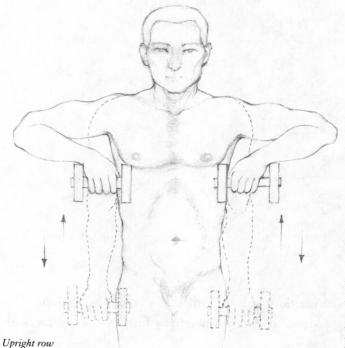

Upright row

7. Upright rows for shoulders and chest. Done standing with knees slightly bent. One- or two-handed depending upon the weight, which is raised from in front of the thighs to the nipple line. Two sets of fifteen reps.

8. Overhead presses for neck and shoulders. Performed standing. Weights are raised from shoulders to extended arm position overhead. Two sets of fifteen reps.

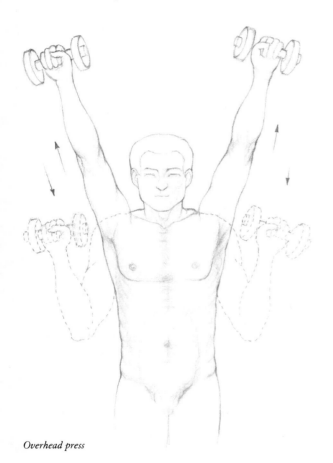

Overhead press

Squat

9. Squats for the quadriceps muscles of the anterior thighs. Performed with or without weights. Knees from slightly bent position to sitting position and return. Two sets of fifteen reps.

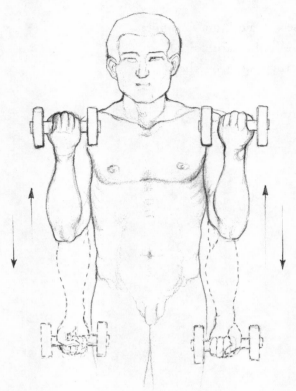

Biceps curl

10. Biceps curls for upper arm. Done with weight held in each hand; can be simultaneous or alternated. Weight is carried from extended to flat position of arm. Two sets of fifteen reps.

The 10/15/20 concept is simplicity itself. It is a compact, time-efficient routine with concrete objectives. Little in equipment or time is necessary, and it is hard to find an excuse to avoid getting started.

The weights will change as your body changes, bringing with the changes a great sense of accomplishment. You don't have to like it to realize immediately how much good you are doing for yourself. Consult any exercise book for details on the safe methods to perform each of these exercises, or better still, treat yourself to a session with a trainer. There are infinite variations, additions, and deletions applicable, and you will soon find your own routine. The important thing is to make physical exercise a part of your life. There is no excuse not to.

SMOKING

I cannot begin even the most cursory discussion of smoking without envisioning readers rolling their eyes and saying, "Not the same old speech again." There is little to add to what we already know of the devastating health risks of smoking. It is your own responsibility to refrain from smoking cigarettes. If you smoke, you must accept and endure the cardiovascular and neoplastic consequences so regularly visited upon the smoker.

In addition to causing life-threatening illnesses, cigarette smoking also affects the skin and the aging process. By causing constriction of the small blood vessels nourishing the skin, smoking acts in much the same way as diabetes. The result is rapid aging of the skin in the form of wrinkling, thinning, and discoloration. The reduction in blood supply is so significant that most plastic surgeons refuse to perform face-lifts on smokers until a period of abstinence is observed, to prevent complications virtually unheard of in nonsmokers.

Habit, and the pleasure of nurturing the habit, are the only reasons to smoke cigarettes. The fear of gaining weight after stopping is based on reality, as is the difficulty of actually breaking the addiction, but both problems are manageable. The evidence is clear to young people, and yet many have taken up smoking just as less well informed prior generations have in the naive past. Perhaps for many of the young, smoking will be a passing fancy and they will be able to extricate themselves before disaster strikes. Most evidence shows decades of smoking are typically required for the negative cardiovascular effects and the threat of cancer. There is little information I know of demonstrating permanent effects of short-term early smoking. Whatever the case, it is better to stop now than tomorrow.

Cigar smoking has returned with a vengeance. There is mixed information about its dangers. The typical cigar smoker doesn't inhale, doesn't keep the wet cigar between his lips, and rarely smokes more than a few cigars a week. These are all circumstances that mitigate risk.

Inhaling smoke, whether intentionally or not, presents the carcinogens to the lungs, where they accumulate and potentially cause cancer. Even secondary smoke has this potential, though measurement is difficult. Therefore smoking in a well-ventilated environment or smoking outside lessens the risk. Cigar and pipe smoking are also associated with lip, mouth, and tongue cancer. There appears to be a linear relationship between the risk and the time the cigar or pipe spends in the mouth, as well as the constancy of the local irritation of smoke. Wet tobacco against the mouth or lip can also cause local cancers and facilitates the absorption of nicotine. In fact, tobacco cured for cigar manufacture is of higher pH than cigarette tobacco and the nicotine in its smoke is more readily absorbed through the mucosal lining of the mouth; the more acidic cigarette smoke must be inhaled for nicotine absorption.

While it is obviously better to avoid smoking altogether, in normal usage cigars appear far less dangerous than cigarettes as a factor in coronary artery disease and cancer. Used sparingly, as seems to be the norm, they may present little health hazard. Still, that is no excuse to start smoking anything at all.

SHAVING

Shaving, chore though it may be, is part of the reason men's faces rarely show the wrinkling that affects middle-aged women. A rich blood supply sustains the hair follicles of the beard, and the facial skin becomes thicker and more resilient. At the surface of this well-nourished skin, shaving provides daily exfoliation, removing patches of loose dead cells and allowing the rotation of a new keratinized layer to the surface. This routine serves men's skin well.

It would be interesting to know if all of this would change appreciably with the exclusive use of electric razors, or in men who didn't shave, or from one cheek to the other. How much benefit is due to the richness of the blood supply and how much to shaving? It would be difficult to ascribe relative values to these factors. Rather, we should simply be pleased to have this hedge against wrinkled cheeks.

A note about **shaving lotions**. There is no value, other than aesthetic, to be found in the use of any of the popular preshave or aftershave lotions. Some shaving creams have silicone or local anaesthetic in the formula to make the shaving easier and painless, but no therapeutic value is implied. What would make sense is a shaving cream incorporating alpha-hydroxy acid. If the chemical and physical properties were compatible one would derive the daily benefits of long-term mild AHA treatments.

ALPHA-HYDROXY ACIDS

Over the last several years, alpha-hydroxy acids have become the hottest thing in skin care, and that makes sense, because they are the first over-the-counter preparations that actually work.

Alpha-hydroxy acids are derived from naturally occurring substances, such as sugarcane, citrus fruit, grapes, and milk. The individual substances include glycolic acid, citric acid, lactic acid, salicylic acid, and some others, depending on the source. The active ingredient is an alpha-hydroxy acid, hence the generic term. There seems little difference between types, so long as preparation and concentration are correct and the substance is properly applied.

The alpha-hydroxy acids are irritants. They work by dislodging the superficial layer of the skin and encouraging a more rapid cell turnover, and they may actually improve the underlying collagen and elastic tissues. The visible results include lightening or eliminating blemishes, improving superficial wrinkles, and reversing elements of sun damage. In teenage skin, alpha-hydroxy acids have been shown to remove debris, alleviate blackheads and whitehead pimples, and smooth irregular areas. For most people the skin becomes generally smoother and healthier-appearing.

AHA is available in many forms and concentrations. There are over-the-counter preparations in the form of creams, lotions, and AHA-moisturizer mixtures. Although the FDA has not placed an upper limit on the concentration available without prescription, most manufacturers have stayed near the 10 percent range. At this level there is felt to be therapeutic value without risk of redness, peeling, flaking, or discoloration.

Most professionals feel a higher concentration than the over-the-counter 10 percent maintenance preparations of AHA should be used for jump-starting the process. This takes the form of a series of AHA applications of increasing concentration from 20 to 70 percent. The object is to achieve the maximal results without the actual peeling. This may sound like something of a contradiction, but much of the value of AHAs resides here. The usual concentrations of these acids, when applied for minutes until a tingling sensation is felt, then neutralized, redden the skin very briefly and do not cause peeling, skin breakdown, or discoloration as is common with other, more traditional peeling agents. There is no downtime at all, and most people see a lightening of blemishes and sun spots, smoothing of the surface of the skin, and amelioration of some fine wrinkles over a period of weeks. There is no risk from sun exposure as there is with Retin-A or other peels, and if these "superficial peels" are not as effective as deeper peels—and they aren't—there is also less risk.

Alpha-hydroxy acid peels will not remove wrinkles, and they will not smooth pockmarks or significantly tighten the skin, but they will smooth the skin, relieve blemishes, and make the skin look and feel better. This is a very low risk option that many men have found beneficial for reversal of superficial skin irregularities and discoloration.

Beyond AHA: Bleaching Creams

When age spots, sun spots, or whatever you choose to call those unsightly dark blemishes about the cheeks and forehead become a problem, the solution requires more than AHA therapy. These discolorations are the curse of sun exposure and age, and though ubiquitous and benign, they are most unpleasant to behold in the shaving mirror.

Among the modalities available to combat them are laser resurfacing, curettage (scraping), peeling and bleaching creams, and tretinoin cream (Renova). Of the above, only bleaching cream is self-administered and complication-free. High-concentration AHA often works at this task, but requires weekly treatment by a physician or nurse. Low-concentration AHA would be slow indeed without the high-concentration start, and would not likely be fully effective. The active ingredient in bleaching creams is hydroquinone. This acts to block the conversion of the amino acid tyrosine to melanin, the skin pigment. The process is not actually bleaching, but rather a devious, well-thought-out scientific process making exquisite use of knowledge of the precursors of melanin. The four months of daily application required before there are visible results may seem long to wait in this world of instant gratification, but it took decades to get those dark spots to begin with.

TRETINOIN

Retin-A is the familiar brand name for tretinoin, a close relative of vitamin A long used in the treatment of acne. The compound was found to reduce the depth of superficial wrinkles, smooth rough skin, and lighten dark spots, and found a far greater life in its new identity. Recently, the FDA permitted the marketing of Renova, a somewhat milder version in an emollient, as a wrinkle treatment. That makes it the first product acknowledged by the government as effective against wrinkles. Produced by the Ortho Pharmaceutical division of Johnson & Johnson, it remains unchallenged. In all likelihood, other tretinoin-based products will be available from other manufacturers, but for now we can use the terms tretinoin and Retin-A or Renova interchangeably.

Repeated studies of patients after several months of nightly tretinoin use show increased thickness of skin previously thinned by sun damage, a smoother surface, and reduced wrinkles. All of these changes are relative, and one should not expect this to be the answer to all the problems of aging, damaged skin. One of the methods of action seems to be increased cell turnover. Studies spanning several years of use fail to show any negative effects, but there is, of course, that Hayflick number staring at us. The question always comes to mind: are we simply hastening the time when cell division will wear out? Or, perhaps, all of this will be reversed by the genetic introduction of telomerase to make the Hayflick concept obsolete.

Tretinoin is applied nightly to newly cleansed skin, then dried for twenty minutes. Initially a period of irritation often occurs, which may last a week or two. This is usually self-limited; if it persists, the treatment should be discontinued. After several months of use the positive effects are noted. For most men, use is limited to the area about the eyelids, with the intention of lightening the color of the skin and improving fine wrinkles.

Throughout the use of tretinoin, the skin must be carefully protected from sunlight.

HUMAN GROWTH HORMONE

Human growth hormone, HGH, is all the rage these days. Many, with some justification, consider it the fountain of youth. Not a statement to be taken lightly, nor was it meant to be. This is a topic of great interest.

In 1990, Dr. Daniel Rudman, leading a group of researchers and clinicians, published a disturbing study in *The New England Journal of Medicine,* the conclusion of which stated, "Diminished secretion of growth hormone is responsible in part for the decrease of lean body mass, the expansion of the adipose tissue mass, and the thinning of the skin that occur in old age."

That probably doesn't mean much to you, but to students of aging the conclusion was less important than the results that led to it. Rudman found that these markers—thinning of the skin, reduced lean muscle mass, and increased fat deposits around the midsection—could be reduced significantly in men from age sixty-one to eighty-one simply by administering growth hormone. Diet, exercise, and other factors were not considered. Later studies showed increased ability to perform a myriad of tasks from stair climbing and lifting and increased mental function and sexual ability, and all this just by increasing growth hormone to the level of the average young male.

This hormone, HGH, is produced by the pituitary gland in the brain and is responsible for normal growth and development in youth. Decreased amounts result in stunted bone growth and reduced stature. To counter this devastating problem in children who failed to grow, purified cadaver growth hormone and later genetically reproduced hormone were administered with great success. As youth passes, the level of circulating HGH decreases markedly, ebbing to near zero in old age. Rudman's findings linked many of the signs of aging to lowered circulating HGH. His proof lay in the reversal of these findings with the physiological administration of HGH. Skin thickened and tightened, lean muscle mass increased, abdominal fat melted away, and vitality returned. Unscientific, anecdotal evidence spoke of a reawakening of sexual prowess, which got everyone's attention.

Early studies had an unacceptably high complication rate, but it was soon discovered that these virtually disappeared with reduced dosage and altered schedules of administration. This shouldn't have been much of a surprise, because the split dosage maintained a hormone level throughout the day that was consistent with the natural state in youth. Among the complications, the most annoying was a debilitating wrist inflammation called carpal tunnel syndrome, and among the most serious were abnormal growth patterns and enlargement of male breasts. The latter two were rare, but severe enough to make one think twice about the wisdom of this therapy.

Complications aside, HGH therapy is very promising, but little further progress has been made. There are some major studies currently in progress, but most of the newer claims are just that—claims made by individuals who have not produced truly scientific evidence and therefore cast a faddist light over the topic. There is reason to believe HGH may reverse elements of heart disease, increase bone density, and reverse or blur the classic markers of old age. It has been found that strenuous exercise and antioxidant intake significantly raise the level of circulation HGH, which may do much to combat aging—another reason that active individuals live longer, healthier lives. If you are questioning whether they live longer, better lives because they are healthier, and not vice versa, join the club. Skepticism is appropriate, but the evidence compels a longer, deeper look.

The advent of Viagra, the new potency pill, has lessened this facet of interest in HGH. There is, however, a great deal of difference between the two. Viagra increases blood supply to the penis, as it was originally intended to do for the heart. The flagging blood supply of impotence is thereby corrected. For normal men there is said to be a significant increase in intensity and duration of erection as well. HGH does not augment the natural state, but is thought to restore youthful sexual function along with removal of the signs of aging. For most men, this would be quite enough.

Do not run out and find someone to provide you with HGH. All of the evidence is yet to surface, and as potent an agent as this is very likely to carry with it some real dangers. Still, this is exciting stuff—like science fiction. Remember the telomere, which controls the biological clock? On January 14, 1998, it passed from conjecture to reality as scientists reported lengthening human cell life with genetic induction of telomerase. It seems very likely that telomerase will be available in the next decade to inhibit cell obsolescence on a clinical level. Add the possibility of reversed aging with the next generation of HGH and who knows. Take good care of yourself, and save for the future—you may live 150 years, and live them well.

DAILY SKIN CARE

Men no longer wince at talk of routine skin care. In fact, they routinely ask about it. Could it be that we feel left out of the billions of dollars spent annually on advertising and promotion, or are we just getting smart? After all, it isn't particularly macho to look old before your time.

Though the chemical and physical processes of aging vary little between the sexes, there are significant differences that warrant alterations in approach. These are based on both sociological stereotypes and anatomy. The best route to understanding the regime of skin care is discussion of the various problems, goals, and effective products. Not all of us have the same problem areas or the same intensity of interest, and flexibility is built in.

Male facial skin is somewhat thicker than female, partly because of the hair follicles of the beard and the supporting rich vasculature. The collagen layer is somewhat thicker as well, and it is unclear whether this is a primary difference or secondary to the increased blood supply. Shaving exfoliates dead cells, and men's cheek skin is generally wrinkle-free. The most prominent wrinkles and folds are found about areas of action of the muscles of facial expression, particularly smile lines outside the eyes and nasolabial folds from the corners of the nose to the corners of the mouth and beyond. No skin care routine can affect the nasolabial folds, and smile lines are reasonably acceptable to most men, even felt to be attractive. Early smile lines are relieved to some degree by the application of tretinoin cream, marketed as Retin-A or Renova. This is a vitamin A derivative, which is applied to the skin surface daily. Most patients report reduced wrinkle depth after several weeks of use. Others report violent irritation or no response at all. The irritation may be an exaggerated positive reaction, and often subsides with lower dosage, moisturizers, or time. Tretinoin seems to work by causing cell turnover and plumping out existing cells. The use of tretinoin will be suggested as it applies to the discussion of particular issues. It is effective in reducing wrinkles, but for the most part it has not been well received by men.

The fine lines and surface irregularities that develop with age are responsive to application of alpha-hydroxy acids, as are the discolorations that arise from age and sun damage. Over-the-counter AHA produces a low-level skin peel after long application at a dilute concentration. Often a series of more concentrated AHA peels administered by a plastic surgeon or dermatologist preceding this daily use is necessary to get the process started.

It takes very little to help prevent the signs of aging and maintain one's skin in the best possible condition—little time or expense, and very little deviation from current practices. It just doesn't make sense not to help yourself look your best. All that is necessary is listed on the following page.

Soap and water
Vitamin C and vitamin E supplements
Sunscreen (SPF 15)
AHA cream
Tretinoin
Moisturizer

The first three items are necessary for everyone, though sunscreen may be a daily necessity only in some climates. The last three, AHA, tretinoin, and moisturizer, are optional. Vitamins C and E, previously covered in depth, play an active role in skin maintenance. They should be part of a daily routine, so at the risk of boring you to death, I'll mention them repeatedly.

A Daily Skin Care Routine

Nothing could be easier.

Before the morning shave, wash your face with soap and water. No matter what your mother told you, soap and water does the job better than any cleansing cream. Prior to shaving, the accumulated cellular debris, ambient pollution, and the residue of yesterday's applications should be removed. The face should be rinsed with warm water. Water slightly above body temperature of 98.6 degrees Fahrenheit feels warm and encourages increased blood flow and vasodilation, cleaning and nourishing the skin from the inside. Hot water is not necessary or desirable, as it may injure the skin.

The natural surface of the skin is slightly acidic, and using a **mild and slightly acidic soap** helps maintain this balance. Soaps like Basis and Dove are gentle and well balanced, as are many others. Avoid soaps with perfumes, or antibacterial soaps, as they are often irritants. If they work for you and you like them, by all means continue. The important points are mildness and pH balance. Gently lather face, neck, and eye area, then wash lather off with copious amounts of warm water.

Shave, then repeat the washing process, this time following the warm rinse with a refreshing cold rinse. The cold water will close down the blood vessels . . . and it feels great. Many men do the preshaving wash in the shower; others shave in the shower as well. The important point is a well-lathered wash before and after shaving. The final wash removes shaving cream and cellular debris.

Toweling dry provides an additional brief exfoliation. It covers areas not shaved and does much to remove heaped-up dead cells from the surface and make the skin look better.

Men rarely complain of facial skin dry enough to require **moisturizers** for relief. The need is more likely to arise in cold dry climates. Northern winters and indoor heating are the culprits. The thought of using moisturizers is a new one to most men, and a word about what they are and how they work is important.

The skin serves to keep the inside environment in and the outside environment out. It is relatively impermeable, with interlocking keratinocytes as the outermost layer. These are dead cells that arise from the living basal layer of the epidermis and make their way to the surface as others are shed. Fresh cells provide a smooth, clear layer, and exfoliation keeps old cells from heaping up. In dry conditions these cells lose some of their moisture and the layer becomes dry, irregular, and even cracked. This does not imply any similar changes in the living cells or the internal aspects of the skin or the body itself. Dryness is a condition of the dead-cell layer of the epidermis. Individuals who manufacture greater quantities of skin oil maintain the moisture of the superficial keratinized cells better than those who produce less oil. Moisturizers mimic the action of the naturally produced skin oils. They are applied to dampened skin and seal the moisture into the keratinized layer. Oil would do the job, as would Crisco, lard, or axle grease. Unfortunately these substances are somewhat crude, may cause severe irritation, and, in the case of lard, attract flies.

All things considered, a more elegant preparation is desirable. Moisturizers are designed to do this job. They are engineered to mimic the natural oils of the skin. They should be allergen-free, perfume-free, invisible when applied, and easily tolerated. Despite what manufacturers claim, moisturizers do nothing to improve the intrinsic nature of the skin. They are either oil- or water-based applications that temporarily trap moisture in the keratinized layer of the skin. The actual moisture content of the skin varies very little, and is not affected by the application of moisturizers. There is no cumulative effect or actual therapeutic value in moisturizers, and they must be applied daily if they are to work. In many ways it is like applying Chap Stick to the lips, and few of us object to that. There is no appreciable difference between moisturizers made of collagen or other scientific-sounding substances and the simplest formulations. Trial and error will lead to the proper product for you. The more expensive moisturizers are not necessarily better. Before you dismiss using moisturizers, try it. Your skin will look and feel better. You can see the difference.

If a moisturizer is required, or desired, splash your face with cool water and apply the moisturizer to the damp skin. A small amount goes a long way; the skin should not be greasy after application. Moisturizer may be used after each washing, though only once a day is required.

Many formulations now include **alpha-hydroxy acid**. The moisturizer serves as a vehicle for the AHA and smoothes the skin and reduces visible flaking from the slight peeling effect of the AHA.

Alpha-hydroxy acid preparations are best applied at night, with or without moisturizer. AHA preparations are invisible, and application takes all of fifteen seconds.

A **sunscreen** is as necessary for men as for women. Ultraviolet radiation is *the* cause of premature aging, and the simple expedient of using a sunscreen will prevent this irreversible damage. There is no excuse not to use it. Before you pat yourself on the back for using sunscreen, think about how often you do, compared with how often you are exposed to casual sun without protection. To be most effective, sunscreen should be applied whenever one ventures into the sun, and for people in southern climates that means every day. If this becomes routine your skin will remain more attractive and age far more slowly. Reflected ultraviolet light from sidewalk, snow, or other surfaces does significant damage, as does driving with open windows or reading on the porch. Sunscreen is not required solely at the beach or on the golf course—we've all learned to use it then. However, northern winters are spent indoors and there is little risk assumed by skipping sunscreen.

In the evening the washing routine is repeated. This removes debris, pollution, old moisturizer, and visible dirt. Some of the sunscreen applied in the morning interacts with surface cells and remains in place despite washing. But this is not enough protection to rely on for the following day. AHA cream or lotion should be applied alone or in a moisturizer vehicle. This is applied to all areas of facial skin, including the lower eyelids and smile lines. If there are specific areas of wrinkling that are bothersome, they can be treated with **tretinoin,** in the form of Retin-A or Renova. This is applied at night, twenty minutes after drying skin thoroughly. If both tretinoin and AHA are being used, the AHA is applied in the morning, tretinoin at bedtime.

Again:
1. **Wash thoroughly with soap and water morning and night.**
2. **Take vitamin C and vitamin E daily.**
3. **Use sunscreen.**
4. **Use AHA and moisturizers as necessary.**
5. **Use tretinoin as necessary.**

Active Intervention Through the Years

So far this book has focused on measures one can take to minimize and forestall the effects of aging on one's appearance. There are, of course, more aggressive procedures designed to reverse the signs of aging, and they vary from minimally invasive to fully surgical. These procedures will be briefly mentioned in this chapter as we predict the toll taken by the decades, and then will be explored in depth in the next chapter, "Antiaging Procedures."

WHAT YOU SEE AT THIRTY-FIVE

For most men there is little change to speak of before the mid-thirties. With a normal lifestyle and routine prevention there should be very minimal changes at this age. There is the dreaded threat of hair loss, which begins for some as early as the twenties, for most by the mid-thirties, for others later, or not at all. This is too charged an issue to deal with in passing and will fill a chapter of its own, where you will learn more than you may care to know about hair loss and hair replacement.

The first signs of aging occur about the eyes, where the finest, thinnest skin is found. Here, through years of squinting, smiling, sun exposure, spice, salt, alcohol, and emotion, the skin swells and shrinks, folds and unfolds in the routines of everyday life. The smiling and squinting etch lines through the action of the orbiculus oculi muscle, a circular muscle that composes the substance of the eyelids. It contracts, crinkling up the skin on the cheeks alongside the eyes. The skin continues to fold repeatedly at the same place, causing collagen breakdown and a wrinkle at the precise folding point determined by the fine attachments of muscle to skin. These wrinkles are barely visible at first but become deeper and more noticeable with time.

Most men accept these smile lines as the natural course of things and are not disturbed by them. There is a sharp, and unfair, distinction between the way signs of age are perceived

Changes visible at age thirty-five

by men and women. For women, the appearance of facial lines, even smile lines, represents the end of a stage of life—the beginning of the end of youth, and the exit from a period in which feminine beauty is graced by youthful perfection. This is not quite the case with men. Though youth is respected, early aging is not feared in the same manner, at the same age level, and with the same intensity. All this is, of course, a sociological phenomenon, and has very little to do with the changes that have actually occurred. There is the overriding perception of maturity and power at every level of the masculine image, although we may prefer a youthful and handsome maturity. So a few smile lines, if that is all we are considering, will not distress most men.

What to do about these lines now that you have taken note of them? The preventive maintenance discussed in the previous chapter will help you avoid making things worse. AHA or tretinoin will help relieve some of these lines. Sunblock and sunglasses will ward off others. Fat transfer may be necessary to reverse the deepest lines, such as the nasolabial folds. If overhanging eyelid skin is manifested early, this is the time to deal with it. It will not cure itself, so get it taken care of and start again at ground zero. Surgically removing the excess skin presents the opportunity to deal with the deepening smile lines as well. This can take the form of simple skin tightening, which will reduce the depth of the lines, or laser or skin peel resurfacing.

Again, the basic rules of prevention should be observed to help maintain the status quo and stop making things worse. This applies at any stage. Measures include the use of sunblock, sunglasses, and an alpha-hydroxy acid preparation, combined with moisturizer or in peel form. These techniques serve well as a first line of defense.

Few men are willing to go to the trouble of applying Retin-A to the smile line area, both because of the nightly effort, which requires a twenty-minute interval between washing and application, and because of the redness often resulting, which women easily cover with makeup. Fewer still choose collagen or fat as a filler in this area.

At the same time, at about age thirty-five to forty, the first signs of skin loosening are noticed. These are usually minimal, and take the form of deepening of the nasolabial fold and the increasing presence of fat under the mandible or a double chin. Both of these situations, if they arise, are best treated early. The depth of the nasolabial folds will only increase with time, and the line at their base will become permanently etched into the skin if it isn't dealt with at a fairly early stage. The method of choice is microsuction of the fat from the overhanging, lateral part of the fold to flatten it somewhat, and injection of the fat removed, or of fat harvested from another site, into the fold itself. This technique is described in depth in the section on procedures. The purpose is to make the high part of the fold lower and the low part higher, thereby leveling the area as much as possible and minimizing the fold and correcting the line developing within it. This is a relatively minor office procedure, well tolerated and with good results. The fat transplant portion of the procedure will have to be repeated six months to a year later, as some 50 to 75 percent of the transplanted fat may be reabsorbed. Twenty percent or more of the fat transplanted in each session seems to find a blood supply and lives permanently at the site. From this you can see that two fat transplants typically result in 50 percent or more permanent correction. Often a third fat transplant may be required. It depends upon the individual, the degree of correction desired, and the technique. Remember, these are transplants of your own living fat cells—from you to you. They are not frozen fat cells, which seem to do little more than act as filler and perhaps set up a small fibrous reaction. The transplantation of fat, or fat injection, or fat transfer, whatever we wish to call it, takes only fifteen minutes, under local anesthetic. There is no pain afterward, but variable amounts of swelling do result, so don't plan to return to work the day of the procedure.

Double chin and plumpness about the jawline are best treated early. The reasons are many. To begin, this problem, when not associated with generalized obesity, is familial. Therefore, it will not disappear on its own, but will increase with the years and gravity, stretch the skin, and become more marked. The solution is microsuction. There are a fixed number of fat cells per square inch in each area. Removal of the fat cells is permanent, and should be done to the point that reflects the overall body look or slightly thinner if appropriate. The optimal time to remove this excess fat is when the skin is still elastic enough to shrink rapidly to fit the underlying structures. Later in life one takes the risk of loose skin resulting. Trading a bag of skin filled with fat for an empty bag of skin is not appealing. For most men the skin remains elastic enough to support the procedure well into their forties, even to age fifty. It varies from individual to individual, and the technique of microsuction even seems to encourage skin shrinkage. In all circumstances, the earlier the better is the rule for this procedure.

The same is true for under-eye bags, which are familial and "seem to have been there forever." These congenital bags are in the family album—they are in the genetic makeup of the individual. You did nothing to cause them, and they are not a sign of aging, but they make one look older and tired nonetheless, and there is nothing that can be done about them but surgery. When performed early, the surgery can be done without any visible scar. This procedure is called transconjunctival blepharoplasty, and it differs from traditional blepharoplasty in the route of access to the fatty pouches. The excess fat is removed through a small incision on the conjunctival membrane, which lines the inside of the lid. The incision heals rapidly and leaves no visible scar. Again, this procedure is best suited for younger individuals, as the skin must shrink after the removal of the offending fatty pouches. This works very, very well in younger people, often into the forties.

When the congenital bags become bothersome is the time to do the operation. As people age there is a loss of elasticity, which usually coincides with wrinkles of the lower lid. For these men, it is necessary to do the standard lower-lid blepharoplasty described in the procedure section. This will remove the bags and the excess skin if there is any, minimize wrinkles, and take up the slack in the skin previously filled by the fatty bags. Lower-lid blepharoplasty is among the most frequently performed cosmetic procedures for the male population. The operation is easy, the results rewarding, and the tiny scar is beneath the lashes, barely visible in a week.

WHAT YOU SEE AT FORTY-FIVE

From forty to forty-five, significant changes occur. Fair-skinned men, as a rule, age earlier than darker-skinned men. The propensity to early changes is entirely genetic, and is primarily inherited among people of northern European descent. This implies absolutely no parallel with general aging and health; it merely reflects the ability of the skin to cope with modern life and ultraviolet light exposure. These men develop deeply lined, craggy faces, with overhanging upper eyelids and lines about the mouth. Darker individuals suffer these first visible signs as a loosening of the skin rather than wrinkling. Whatever the case, the changes become significant in the middle to late forties.

Smile lines increase in number and depth. Nasolabial lines and folds become more pronounced in those liable to develop them, and a loosening of the skin along the jawline and under the jaw begins. The skin itself continues to look youthful in the areas of daily shaving, where the exfoliating has served as a daily mini-peel. Little intervention is necessary. If the eyelid skin has stretched and redundant skin is noticeable, one might begin to consider blepharoplasty, the surgical removal of excess skin, puffiness, and wrinkles from about the eyelids. If smile lines and wrinkles alone are the problem, laser resurfacing might be considered, but the procedure results in several weeks of profound redness, which most men tolerate poorly. Alpha-hydroxy acid peels will help to a lesser degree, and offer the advantage of no telltale redness. The two procedures, laser resurfacing and AHA peels, are, unfortunately, in no way equivalent in results; the laser resurfacing reverses the problem, while the AHA ameliorates it.

Changes visible at age forty-five

At forty-five there may be some concern about the deepening frown line between the eyebrows. This can be simply dealt with at the same time as blepharoplasty by corrugator muscle resection to stop future unnecessary frowning and fat transfer to correct the present problem.

WHAT YOU SEE AT FIFTY TO FIFTY-FIVE

Fifty—no fun even saying it. The good news is that by this time of life most men have had significant achievement in their professional and private lives, and this certainly takes the edge off. More important, in today's society a man of fifty or fifty-five, or sixty, should feel young and powerful, with nothing but common sense to keep him from all youthful pursuits.

Still, the signs of aging are pretty much unavoidable by fifty-five. Here too there exists a great spectrum of individual variation. For some, the clear signs of aging manifest themselves as etched lines among lean features, manly, attractive, but clearly mature beyond youth. Even this sort of situation can be improved. Much can be done, much can be minimized, as long as one maintains an element of reality and good taste. Can a man of fifty look gracefully fortyish? Yes, that is very possible. It is only when the reaches of common sense are exceeded that one takes on an unattractive, artificial look, and that must be avoided at all costs. There are some stigmata of aging that cannot be reversed, and these must be accepted. A middle-aged man with hair poorly dyed jet black, thin skin pulled taut, and eyes sad-looking from excessive skin removal, trying to be what he is not, is pitiable. The objective is to be the best-looking, most virile man of indeterminate years that it is possible to be, not to be an artificial man.

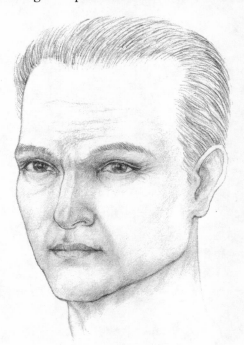

Changes visible at age fifty-five

In the years from fifty to fifty-five, most men develop varying degrees of redundant skin of the upper eyelids, resulting from collagen and elastin breakdown and from gravity. The changes are often accelerated by lifestyle and sun. The lower eyelids usually show wrinkles, some excess skin, and pouches. Smile lines are indelible. When the stretched, excess upper-eyelid skin becomes hooding, it is not only unattractive but annoying, often interfering with vision. This is not due to stretching of the eyelid skin alone, for at this point loosening of the forehead skin and descent of the eyebrows begins to add to the mix. All of these situations can be easily corrected.

Blepharoplasty will remove the excess skin and bags from the lower lids, lessen smile lines, and remove excess skin and fat pads from the upper lids. When necessary the eyebrows can be elevated by any of several means, which are covered in detail in the procedures section. They include eyebrow lift and forehead lift. Often corrugator resection is indicated at the same time to correct the frown line between the eyebrows. Horizontal lines of the forehead deepen. Few men are seriously bothered by this development, which is probably a good thing, as most effective remedies require incisions in the scalp, which will not necessarily be hidden by hair as is likely to be the case with women.

By this age, nasolabial folds have become heavier in all but the thinnest faces. Neck skin is taut in the chin-up position but lax when the head is set normally straight ahead. Two vertical bands appear at the front of the neck. These represent the leading edge of the platysma muscles of the left and right neck, which have become lax within the skin and are no longer joined together at the midline. A hint of jowls is seen. Small pouches develop alongside and slightly below the corners of the mouth. Dark areas develop typically on the forehead and cheeks because of repeated sun damage. By this point the hair loss has stabilized.

The nasolabial folds may be treated very effectively by microsuction and fat transfer. These procedures will be useful for the small pouches beside the mouth as well. Loose skin beneath the jawline and platysma bands must be dealt with surgically. The appropriate procedures include local fat removal and skin and muscle tightening via an incision under the chin. This is a relatively minor procedure and usually yields dramatic results. The downside is a scar under the chin. Some version of a neck-lift or face-lift may be necessary in more severe cases. The decision at this juncture is which procedure best addresses the problems being considered. Slightly loose submental (under-the-chin) skin and early jowls do not require a face-lift when microsuction and local procedures will do. On the other hand, deep nasolabial folds, jowls, and loose neck skin and platysma muscle cannot be corrected through a small under-the-chin incision. The procedure must be appropriate to the problem. Here nothing can substitute for the experience of the surgeon. He must recommend the solution.

WHAT YOU SEE AT SIXTY TO SIXTY-FIVE

At sixty-five the cumulative changes of the past are evident, and progress slowly with the loss of vitality and elasticity of the skin. Eyelid skin is stretched. Nasolabial folds, cheek pouches, and jowls increase. Loose skin of the neck worsens. Subcutaneous fat padding of the face falls with gravity, and a slight downward cant of the mouth corners may be noted.

These changes can be addressed only by face-lift and eyelid surgery. At this stage of life the procedure can result in correction of much of the laxity, but not elimination of wrinkles and deep lines. Fat padding beneath the skin can be replaced into its more youthful position. Skin will fit the underlying facial structure far better, and a natural, more youthful, but mature appearance will result.

Men in this age group who have undergone various of the antiaging procedures in the past will exhibit fewer and less severe signs of aging. Often they choose further surgery based on the success enjoyed with the initial procedures. Secondary face-lifts are usually modest refreshers, aimed at specific trouble spots.

Changes visible at age sixty-five

WHAT YOU SEE BEYOND SIXTY-FIVE

Here individual variations—genetic predisposition, lifestyle, general health, and socio-economic factors—play an enormous role. At sixty-five some men are old. At fifty-five some men are old, but the watershed area seems to be sixty-five and beyond. The physical changes of the face are no longer dramatic. There are a few more wrinkles, the earlobes stretch, the tip of the nose drifts downward and thickens. Folds thicken and jowls increase. Skin-surface changes, like broken blood vessels and discolorations, increase as aging persists. But this is not the rule. Some men manage to remain youthful-looking into their seventies, and are taken for fifteen or twenty years younger. We all know many such individuals, and with proper care, and intervention where necessary, most of us can be among them. There is a reason that men with more education and a greater level of affluence appear far younger than the general population. Up to now, each of us has been unable to influence the genetic unfolding of his predispositions. But with affluence and education comes good medicine, good advice, exercise, skin care, peer pressure, and moderation, all of which serve the individual well.

Those men currently in their fifties or younger can do much to ensure vigorous good looks at sixty-five and beyond. Diet, exercise, antioxidants, and even sunblock remain crucial. Antiaging cosmetic surgery procedures can banish loose skin, and within the brackets of male maturity, age can be just a number.

At sixty-five or seventy, virtually no successful man would consider himself old. Nor should he. We have made great strides toward longevity and good health in the past half century, and that is only the beginning. Cosmetic surgery and its related disciplines are tools to help make the outside look as healthy as the inside continues to be.

Time passes and we all actually do grow old. Doing it gracefully is within your power.

Antiaging Procedures

This is a big topic and rather difficult to circumscribe. A great deal of overlap exists between general cosmetic procedures and antiaging procedures. Similar techniques are employed, and the procedures are first cousins. For our purposes an attempt is made to categorize them for ease of reference, but the overlap is confusing. For example, hair replacement is not considered an antiaging procedure, but for most men hair loss occurs with maturity and is treated because it makes men feel as if they look old. Hence the unclear line. The procedures discussed in this chapter address the problems raised in the decade-by-decade overview just completed.

DEALING WITH WRINKLES AND SAGGING

Microsuction, collagen injections, fat transfers, laser resurfacing, implant fillers, and other minimally invasive techniques are the first line of defense. They are designed to deal with early changes resulting in deepening nasolabial folds, frown lines, wrinkles, early jowls, and loss of the clean contours of the jawline.

Collagen is the primary protein substance of the skin. Its destruction or denaturing results in thinning of the skin, folds, wrinkles, depressions, and sagging. Among the many causes for these changes are the chemical denaturing due to oxidation by free radicals, sun damage, gravity, and constant and repetitive muscle movements, such as frowning, smiling, and all the little things that make our faces human and expressive. These changes are among the earliest visible signs of aging.

For years the primary method of correction was injection of silicone, which proved troublesome, sometimes unpredictable, and impossible to reverse. These and other complications of the method forced the FDA to ban its use. The Collagen Corp. of Palo Alto, California, pioneered the use of injectable collagen as a tissue filler. The source of this collagen is bovine skin, which happens to differ very little in protein makeup from human collagen. Therefore, the purified product is very well tolerated by humans, and is associated with very few allergic reactions. Over the years the product has become easier to use and somewhat longer-lasting, but the nature of the substance is that it usually dissipates within six months. That is bad, because it means treatments must be repeated frequently, and they are costly. However, the fact that the substance is not permanent gives a margin of safety not available with silicone usage.

Injectable collagen seems to perform best in the fine lines about the mouth, the nasolabial folds, and the frown lines between the eyebrows. Misplaced injections and the rare allergic reactions are reported, but the transient nature of the substance make them somewhat self-limited and relatively easy to deal with.

The injection is via a very fine needle. Multiple pinpricks are necessary, but anesthesia is not required. A small amount of local swelling accompanies the injections, but it rapidly subsides. Prior to use a skin test is necessary to isolate and protect those with obvious allergy.

Collagen, marketed as Zyplast, is far and away the most popular of the injectable substances used to fill wrinkles and folds, but the use of fat transfers is rapidly increasing and in many circumstances is far superior.

Fat transfers involve removing small amounts of fat from one part of the body and implanting it by injection into a fold or wrinkle in another part. The immediate advantage is that there are no foreign substances involved. One's own fat is moved from where it exists in excess to where it is needed.

Transplanted fat cells that come in contact with a blood supply have the ability to live permanently at their new site. The remainder, having not established blood supply, remain as filler for periods of up to six months, being gradually mobilized and removed by the body, not unlike what happens to injectable collagen.

The procedure is an easy one, and is usually performed under local anesthesia alone. A site for fat donation is identified, usually the abdomen, hips, or thighs, and the fat is removed with a syringe. After being centrifuged to separate out liquids, the fat cells are injected into the new site. All this takes about fifteen minutes. The limitations of fat transfer are imposed by the nature of the technique. Since the objective is to provide the greatest possibility of fat cell survival, a relatively large-caliber needle is used in an effort to avoid crushing the cells through a smaller aperture. Although this does not necessarily imply discomfort, it does mean that fine lines cannot be treated. The technique is most effective in deep lines and folds like the nasolabial fold and frown lines between the eyebrows. Fat transfer is particularly useful in correcting the downward lines that develop at the corners of the mouth and give one the appearance of frowning or displeasure.

For men, even more than for women, for whom fine lines are more of a problem, fat transfer has become the early procedure of choice. With increasingly sophisticated techniques, the percentage of permanent "take" has risen dramatically. Though the procedure

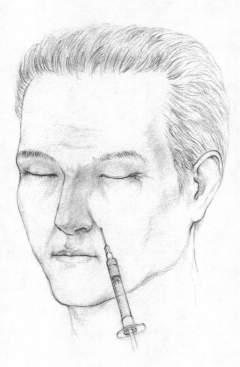

Fat transfer to the nasolabial fold

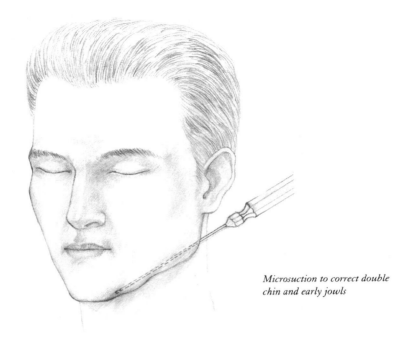

Microsuction to correct double chin and early jowls

is a bit more involved and time-consuming than collagen implants, one can return to work the next day, usually without signs of treatment, and with the possibility of permanent correction. Two or three sessions over a year or two are required before the outcome can be accurately evaluated.

A number of other injectable substances have been tried over the years, and have been virtually abandoned. Collagen and fat transfers remain the two viable choices. A new collagen implant has been recently introduced based on collagen produced from specimens of one's own skin propagated in the laboratory. While this has promise, it doesn't offer the permanence of fat transfers, and it requires surgical harvesting of skin to send to the laboratory.

Solid implants of various materials offer another means of filling folds and deep lines. The newest of these are the use of Gore-Tex threads or tapes and Soft Form, a strawlike device of Gore-Tex produced by the Collagen Corp. Both methods are based on the placement of a relatively inert foreign body beneath the fold as filler, and the ingrowth of cells to stabilize, anchor, and soften the result. Both appear successful, and in selected cases are well received. The downside includes the possibility of being able to feel the implants and occasionally seeing their outline. These are said to be exceptions to the rule, and though the use of these new techniques has been limited, they offer the promise of another useful tool.

For many years plastic surgeons have used strips of fascia and dermis to fill deeper folds and augment lips and skin defects. Though this may offer permanent correction, it requires surgical harvesting. Therefore the technique has been relegated to surgical procedures and is out of the realm of the quick fix.

Microsuction is a very useful procedure for treating early jowls, double chin, fat pockets about the mouth, and heavy nasolabial folds. This procedure can be done under local anesthesia, with sedation, and utilizes a tiny incision, usually under the chin, through which a two- to three-millimeter suction catheter is introduced and excess fat removed. The area becomes flatter and tighter, and the results are usually quite good.

BLEPHAROPLASTY

Blepharoplasty is plastic surgery of the eyelids. Eyelid lift or eyelid plasty mean the same thing. Overhanging skin of the upper eyelids, wrinkled eyelid skin, and lower-eyelid bags are treated by the various types of blepharoplasty.

For men, one of the most frequent reasons for visiting a plastic surgeon is baggy lower eyelids. Correctly or not, one associates this condition with fatigue, drinking, aging, and general dissipation. Actually, the cause is more likely allergy, fluid retention, or heredity, but for most people the symptom does increase with lack of sleep and alcohol. For some the puffy, baggy lower lid is always present and does not reflect lifestyle. Unfortunately, that means little in terms of other people's perception and one may seem to be what one is not.

With aging, lower-lid bags are usually accompanied by some element of puffiness and overhang of the upper lid skin, and so the conditions are often treated simultaneously. Before deciding on a course of action the plastic surgeon and the patient must be clear about the objectives of surgery. Communication is always a critical part of the procedure, and more so when the goals of the procedure differ so widely between men and women. Most women want all the excess skin of the upper and lower lids removed, puffiness corrected, and wrinkles eliminated as completely as possible. They often first notice the overhanging skin very early, usually during the daily task of applying eye makeup. Men notice this excess skin much later, and they care less. When the upper lids are the problem, it has usually reached the point where the lids feel heavy at day's end, or actually interfere with vision. More often, the condition has been brought to their attention by someone else. Men rarely

Incision for treatment of bags of the lower eyelids

ask that every wrinkle and fold be eliminated, and this is fortunate, as a tiny bit of retained excess skin of the upper lids serves as a perfect hiding place for the fine surgical scar that women hide with eye makeup in the early postoperative period. The lower-lid scar disappears far earlier and doesn't present a problem.

Bags of the lower eyelids are more commonly noted by men, and in my practice, at least, lower eyelids are more frequently treated surgically than upper eyelids. The procedure is fairly simple and straightforward.

The puffiness is caused by pockets of fat beneath the orbicularis oculi, the muscle that circles the eye in intimate contact with the skin and composes a substantial portion of the lid. When the muscle weakens and becomes looser, or the fat pockets enlarge or swell with fluid retention, the muscle no longer fully restrains the fat pockets, and visible bags result. In the case of hereditary puffiness of the lower lids, excessive fat is always present, and it becomes more prominent with fluid retention and with the years.

The objective of surgery is the removal of the excess fat and creation of a normal contour of the lower lid. As a side benefit, once the excess fat is removed the lower lids will no longer swell with allergy of fluid retention as they did in the past.

The procedure is typically performed either through a very fine incision beneath the lashes or from an incision inside the eyelid. The first is the most traditional method; it has been employed for more than fifty years. The operation is usually performed in a private clinic or ambulatory surgery center, under sedation and local anesthetic. Through the incision beneath the lashes the fat pockets are identified and the excess is carefully trimmed. Here one must take care not to remove fat too aggressively, or a hollow look may result. I have always instructed young surgeons to be conservative with this maneuver. If too little fat is removed, the oversight can be remedied with a minor procedure. Correcting excessive fat removal is far more difficult.

Once the excess fat is removed, the lid skin is trimmed. This is necessary if one wishes to reduce lower-lid wrinkles and loose skin. It is made more important with the removal of the fatty bags, which had formerly filled and puffed out the skin and have been left somewhat loose and empty. Trimming of the skin is always done carefully and conservatively. Removing a strip of only two or three millimeters is usually enough. If the surgeon is too aggressive and removes too much skin, the lower lid will be pulled down from its normal position, revealing too much of the white of the eye. This condition is unattractive and annoying, but correctable. Sometimes just the swelling from surgery can cause a temporary version of this problem, but this is self-limited and resolves. After the skin is trimmed, the incision is closed with a very fine nylon suture woven beneath the skin and appearing at the ends of the incision as a whisker, or with sutures through the skin. Neither method leaves permanent marks, and the resulting scar soon becomes skin-colored and virtually invisible.

If one chooses to have the bags removed from inside the eyelid, there is no visible scar at all, and for this reason this technique has become quite popular. The same sedation and local anesthesia are employed, and the incision at the base of the inside of the lower lid can be made with a scalpel, laser, or cautery knife. It makes no difference which instrument is used as long as the surgeon is experienced at the procedure.

This incision is made through the lining of the lid, called the conjunctiva, to reach the fat beneath it—hence the name subconjunctival blepharoplasty. The fat pockets are found and the fat trimmed. No sutures are necessary, as the wound heals quickly and invisibly. The procedure is very well tolerated and very successful, and is constantly being oversold by plastic surgeons. But subconjunctival blepharoplasty alone is not always the appropriate choice. Except for the youngest patients, when significant fat is removed an excess of skin results. This must be dealt with or skin folds and wrinkles result. Often the answer is laser resurfacing done with the subconjunctival blepharoplasty. This procedure removes the surface skin layer, resulting in a tighter and smoother result. The problem for most men is the several weeks of red, discolored skin associated with laser resurfacing. This is often quite acceptable to women, who routinely cover the area with makeup until normal color returns. Most men are uncomfortable with this solution, and would prefer the small external incision beneath the lashes, which allows fat and skin removal and becomes rapidly invisible.

When significant excess skin and puffiness of the upper eyelid exists, it is dealt with by direct excision of the offending skin, usually leaving just enough remaining excess to hide the resultant scar. This strategy avoids the need for makeup coverage in the early stages and yields the natural result favored by most men. Sutures for upper-lid blepharoplasty are woven under the skin and are removed easily on about the third day.

The most usual indication for upper-lid blepharoplasty is cosmetic improvement, but some individuals have a functional impairment of vision caused by overhanging upper eyelid skin. This condition is called ptosis of the upper lid. Its causes may be heredity, loss of elasticity, repeated swelling of allergy, or stretching or weakening of the muscle responsible

The broken line indicates excision of excess upper eyelid skin.

for lifting the eyelid, as in such diseases as myesthenia gravis. When the levator muscle stretches or tears, internal sutures are placed in the muscle to shorten or tighten it. If the problem results from inelastic skin, simple skin excision is often all that is necessary. When the cause is neuromuscular illness, the usual treatment is nonsurgical.

Other than the internal tightening, ptosis repair is externally similar to blepharoplasty, and it completely reverses the problem through the same fine incision.

Upper-lid blepharoplasty may be performed alone but is usually done in combination with lower-lid surgery. Whether the procedure involves upper or lower lids alone or uppers and lowers together doesn't affect the postoperative period at all. There are forty-eight to seventy-two hours of significant swelling. Sutures are removed on the third day, and swelling and discoloration disappear over the next few days. Most men take a week away from work. By this time most of the signs of surgery have disappeared, though it is not unusual to have a persistent point of discoloration or two requiring coverage. The following week all normal activities may be resumed. More than half of blepharoplasty patients have temporary disruption of normal tear production after blepharoplasty, and the postoperative use of eyedrops is recommended. What little postoperative pain occurs is controlled completely by the use of iced compresses over the first twenty-four hours. The ice also helps control swelling and bruising, so it is a must for the first postoperative day. Most patients find it very soothing and continue the applications longer. Rarely does a patient report needing more than the mildest analgesic.

When the **vertical frown lines** between the eyebrows are a problem they can be easily dealt with through the upper-eyelid incision, or if upper-eyelid blepharoplasty is not being done, through a half-inch incision in a crease of the upper lid near the nose. The deep wrinkling is, in large measure, caused by action of the corrugator muscle, which courses parallel to the eyebrow and inserts in the skin over the nose. When the muscle contracts, it shortens and wrinkles the skin between the eyebrows. Cutting this small muscle weakens most of this action, and combined with the use of fat transfer to fill in the existing crease, the problem can be largely reversed. Some numbness in the area is often reported, because of injury to a tiny sensory nerve in the eyebrow.

The safety, minimal discomfort, and excellent results of blepharoplasty make it among the most popular procedures performed worldwide. Fees for upper- and lower-lid blepharoplasty together average about $5,000 to $8,000, half that if only uppers or lowers are done. Corrugator resection to correct frown lines costs from $2,000 to $3,500, usually including the fat transfer.

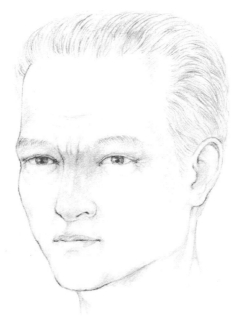

Vertical frown lines between the eyes

TURKEY NECKS AND DOUBLE CHINS

This will get your attention!

Although hardly scientific terms, these are the issues that often send men of middle age and beyond to consult the plastic surgeon. What better description for the loose, wrinkled skin of the jawline and neck than "turkey neck"? It is unaesthetic, impossible to hide, and usually the most glaring example of loss of skin elasticity on the body. Many men see this problem developing in their forties, with rapid progression over the next ten years. A bit of extra eyelid skin and a few deep wrinkles and folds have nothing near the depressing effect of these dewlaps of skin on a man's self-image. Suddenly you look old. This may in no way reflect the condition of your health in general or your actual age. It simply looks old, and few men leading active lives are willing to put up with it. If your father had a turkey neck, it's a good bet that you will too.

Happily, there are many techniques to help dispatch the problem to memory. They vary from very simple to more involved. All are directed at eliminating the loose hanging skin under the jaw and are based on an understanding of the anatomy of the area and the underlying causes.

For the most part the skin of the neck can be thought of as having two layers—the skin itself, and the underlying platysma muscle. The layers are bound together quite closely, and when one loosens, so does the other. This is different from the rest of the face, where there is a loose layer of fat separating the undersurface of the skin from the muscles beneath it. Therefore, it helps to think of neck skin and the muscle beneath as an anatomical unit. Certainly the skin can stretch without the muscle, and vice versa, but they are closely related, and both are treated.

In youth, the platysma muscles, covering the left and right sides of the face, meet at the midline. With aging, the leading edges of these muscles become slack and separate. This is seen as the two vertical bands running from the chin to the chest. Between these muscles there is often a pocket of fat. Over the years the skin of the neck loosens over the muscle. At first this is seen as a little excess when the chin is held down. Soon it hangs even when the jaw is held high. For some this is a hereditary or structural condition, unrelated to aging.

Up to a point there is simply loosening of the skin and muscle from the underlying structures, not actual excess. Beyond that point there is actually more skin than is needed to allow the chin to be raised. Sometimes the problem is related primarily to collections of fat

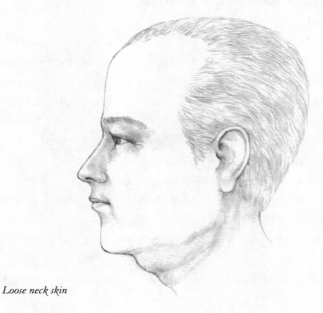

Loose neck skin

on the neck without a marked loss of elasticity. The situation must be evaluated carefully before a surgical plan can be formulated. There are options for each situation.

A fatty double chin may seem like a horrible problem, but is the easiest of the situations to correct. The tendency is hereditary, and the actual double chin may be noted as a teenager. It gets worse over the years. Microsuction is a simple and expedient solution. Under mild sedation and local anesthesia, a small suction catheter is introduced via a quarter-inch incision under the chin. The fat is suctioned out in a fanlike pattern and along the midline. The undersurface of the skin is abraded in the process, and this seems to encourage a bit of tightening. A compressive elastic bandage is worn for three days, and shortly thereafter the result can be seen. Because of the inherent elasticity of youthful skin, the earlier the problem is addressed the better the result. Sometimes there is significant excess skin even in younger men. This is treated by extending the incision under the chin and suturing the platysma muscle bands together. This recontours the neck. The skin draped over the platysma muscle will shrink and conform. But this simple procedure is limited to younger men in whom the skin retains significant elasticity. Less elasticity or more loose skin requires consideration of the following procedures.

Loose skin and muscle bands, those two vertical bands on either side of the midline of the neck, require a different approach than simply microsuction. Moderate looseness can be dealt with by an incision under the chin, through which the extent of the platysma muscle is visualized. The muscle bands are sewn together into their tight youthful position, excess fat is removed, and sometimes excess skin is resected at the incision site under the chin.

This is an extremely useful and relatively simple procedure. After surgery a bulky compressive dressing is worn for a few days to allow the redraped skin to adhere to the tightened muscle, but downtime is limited, and the procedure is very popular because of its success.

There are technical limits to what this simple procedure can accomplish, which may be expanded by altering the nature of the incision. In circumstances of marked skin excess, a Z-shaped incision allows aggressive skin removal; more often, a small "T" is required. This T-shaped incision allows most of the excess skin to be removed with a relatively small scar. The underlying platysma muscle bands are tightened or a portion actually removed. The combination offers a fairly substantial result with limited surgery.

The resulting scar from the T-shaped or Z-shaped excision is very visible in the early postoperative period but is surprisingly less obvious with time. These procedures are easily tolerated, require little in lifestyle restrictions, and are quite effective.

When the problem of loose neck skin is more severe, or a more dramatic result is desired, the approach changes. For the most complete elimination of loose skin the direct approach to the muscle bands is combined with a neck-lift. This is performed via incisions in the crease behind the ears, which continues into the hairline. Through these incisions the skin of the neck is elevated and redraped, removing the excess as completely as possible. An incision is made under the chin as well, through which the platysma muscle is tightened, as described above.

This neck-lift, or lower face-lift, is more extensive than the simple direct approach and requires ten days of restricted activities, with gradual return to physical activities and athletics thereafter. It offers the most complete reversal of the problem, but there is more downtime and a higher incidence of complications. Male facial skin has the deep dermal blood supply necessary to support the beard, and in the course of the neck-lift there is a greater likelihood of postoperative collection of blood, or hematoma, beneath the skin than there is in women. This is the

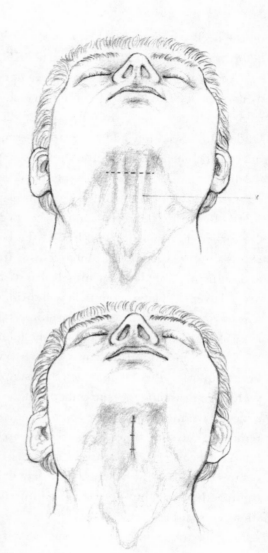

Top, incision for tightening platysma bands.
Bottom, sutures in the platysma muscle beneath the skin.

most frequently reported complication, and though it may happen some 5 percent of the time, there is usually only a small accumulation requiring no therapy. Substantial problems are rare, and the overall results are excellent. Fees for a neck-lift vary between $5,000 and $10,000. Fees for direct skin excision and muscle tightening are appreciably lower.

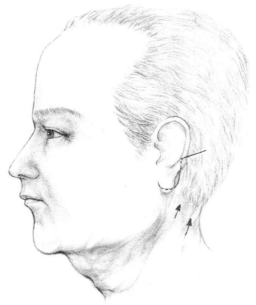

Neck-lift. Note the incision behind the ear.

In the face of high expectations there must be an understanding of the reality of the situation. The skin has lost elasticity enough to hang loosely about the neck, and the operation removes the excess and redrapes the skin neatly over underlying structures, allowing enough skin for movement. But you must understand that the operation does not return elasticity to the skin, and since there must be enough skin to allow you to raise the chin, there will always be a bit of slack when your chin is lowered. Surgeons understand this and compensate for it as much as possible, but you must look normal and be able to move normally, and if that means a bit of laxity, it must be accepted. Most men have no difficulty with this, and are delighted with their graceful new look.

FACE-LIFT

"Face-lift" is a wonderfully descriptive term. The word picture is evocative enough to have entered the vernacular for the rejuvenation of everything from storefronts to menus. Plastic surgeons like the terms **rhytidectomy**, **rhytidoplasty**, and **facialplasty**, which mean wrinkle removal, wrinkle molding, and facial molding, respectively. But the operation does not really remove or mold wrinkles, and although it does mold the face, I think "face-lift" is by far the best term. There are no secret meanings, and everyone gets the picture.

As complex as the aging process is, it brings about predictable changes, primarily wrinkling and loss of elasticity. The individual manifestations may be loose, hanging skin of the cheeks, jowls, and neck, deep nasolabial folds, deep "marionette lines" from the corners of the mouth to the jawline, overhanging upper-eyelid skin, baggy lower lids, and deep smile lines and facial wrinkles. Men get a break here, because the rich blood supply sustaining the beard and the constant exfoliation of shaving seem to protect them from the road map of facial lines that afflicts many middle-aged women. The fair-skinned and sun-exposed are more likely to develop such facial wrinkles, but as a rule men age more gently in this respect. Smile lines occur as often and as deeply as in women, but men rarely find them objectionable. The conditions that concern men are those caused primarily by loss of elasticity, resulting in loose, ill-fitting skin, simply an extension of the process causing jowls and turkey neck. If the lower half of the face and neck were not affected, few men would be bothered enough to consider face-lift. The process leading to the changes is insidious and inexorable. Everything seems fine, and then one day, there they are. Except for the damage done by weight fluctuation and the sun, the changes an individual can expect can be predicted by glancing at the family album. Basic physical properties such as these are genetically determined, and we tend to age in the same fashion as our parents.

As I have said, men generally deal rather well with the odd wrinkles and smile lines. What we do not suffer lightly is the ill-fitting skin that makes us feel old. If the changes are severe enough to require action, it must be in the form of a face-lift. Nothing else does the job—not laser resurfacing, not chemical peels, not acupuncture face-lifts, not sheep embryo injections.

The operation is designed to raise the stretched, redundant skin of the face and neck and replace in its former position. Often the condition includes laxity of the platysma muscles, which extend from the neck upward to the cheek. The procedure requires an incision from the temporal hairline, in front of the ear, around the tip of the earlobe, and up behind the ear, as in the neck-lift.

The incision gives access to the underlying structures, so that they and the skin above can be reoriented, and it differs from the incision used in the female version because of the presence of the beard. A hairless space exists between the beard and the ear. To preserve a normal appearance, this space must not be obliterated, and that presents a bit of a problem, as the incision must therefore be in front of this hairless strip and in direct

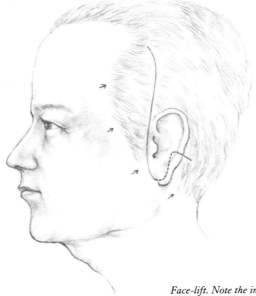

Face-lift. Note the incision within the hairline and behind the ear. Arrows indicate the direction of pull.

view. Luckily, healing in this area is excellent, and the scar fades and virtually disappears with time. However, it is noticeable in the weeks after surgery and must be covered with makeup. In some cases the scar remains raised or red. This problem can be dealt with by laser resurfacing or scar revision, and a satisfactory outcome is the rule. Nonetheless, one must be aware of this possibility before surgery. In the sideburn years of the 1970s, men wore their hair long enough to comb over any problem that might arise, and that is an option for some. For women, the hairless skin of the cheek allows the incision to be hidden inside the ear, which is an advantage.

The SMAS (superficial musculo-aponeurotic system), a tough fascial continuation of the platysma in the cheek, is tightened, relieving much of the heavy nasolabial fold of the cheek and jowls. Microsuction removes excess fat, and the skin is gently redraped in the new position. Great care must be taken to avoid a pulled look. The result must be natural, even if that means leaving a bit of a fold or laxity. The objective is not teenage-tight skin, but the clean, graceful appearance of a good-looking grown man. Anything else results in a caricature.

Men who undergo face-lifts usually need their eyes done as well, and the procedures are routinely performed at the same time. The operation is usually performed on an ambulatory basis. Anesthesia includes sedation and local—rarely full general—anesthetic. Men are likely to be more concerned with the possibility of pain than women, who claim the human race would disappear if we had to bear children. But if we are more apprehensive before surgery, we routinely deal with the postop period like men, while women tend to agonize over every blemish.

Because the fine sensory nerve endings in the skin are separated at surgery, there is a temporary relative numbness that makes the postoperative course painless. Swelling and discoloration last through the first week, and most men return to work from ten days to two weeks after surgery. Possible complications are legion, and vary from serious to annoying, most often being nothing more than minor collections of blood under the skin or temporarily visible scars. Still, possible complications must be discussed with the surgeon prior to surgery. Fees for a facelift range from $7,500 to $15,000. When blepharoplasty is done as well, fees increase accordingly.

Other Cosmetic Procedures

Numerous procedures fall beneath the umbrella of cosmetic surgery but outside the strictly antiaging category. The procedures covered here are the most frequently performed, most talked about, or most misunderstood.

Those that are most sought after are very popular indeed. Heading the list (no pun intended) is **hair transplantation**, a procedure potentially applicable to more than half of the world's adult male population. Thinning hair is ubiquitous, and most cultures attach at least marginal emotional significance to the presence of hair—and to its absence. All men would prefer to have a full head of hair than not, and the search for a quick fix has been the seed of many fortunes. From Samson to the soundstages of Hollywood, male hair has been associated with good looks and virility in much the same emotionally charged manner as large breasts have become symbolic of female sexuality. Nothing could be further from reality in either instance, yet nothing could be more deeply etched in the collective perception of society. In fact, male hair loss has been associated with excessive circulating testosterone, the very nectar of manhood. Try selling that! Attempts at treating male-pattern baldness over the years have occasionally focused on injecting female hormones into the bald scalp to encourage hair growth. That these treatments have not been very successful is beside the actual point, which is that baldness does not in any way reflect upon virility or indicate accelerated aging. It is a simple genetic fact of life, amplified in meaning by society. It must be dealt with for its effect on our lives and with a critical dose of common sense.

Other very popular procedures include **liposuction**, particularly liposuction of the abdomen and the "love handles." Over the past ten years this has become perhaps the most frequently performed procedure for men. As with hair transplantation, the actual numbers are difficult to ascertain because so many physicians, trained and not, have been performing the operation. A low guess would be something in the range of 150,000 cases yearly in the United States alone. Reasons for this popularity include the ubiquitous nature of the problem, the ease with which the procedure is tolerated, and its success. Other areas in which liposuction is popular for men include the neck and jawline.

Rhinoplasty or **nasoplasty** is a procedure quite frequently requested by males of all ages. It can be used for teenage improvement or as an adjunct to antiaging techniques. Most people are familiar with a wealth of secondhand stories but have little understanding of the procedure as practiced today.

Surgery for protruding ears, called **otoplasty**, is common for both males and females, and not limited to the childhood years. The procedure is infrequently performed compared with liposuction, but invaluable when necessary.

Gynecomastia, despite its feminine-sounding name, is a very male problem. It is the abnormal enlargement of the male breast. The cause is usually hormonal, and it results in enlargement of the actual breast tissue and often the surrounding fat. The problem is a very visible one, and the surgical result is dramatic and satisfying. The incidence of gynecomastia is small, but its impact on the men afflicted is substantial.

Implants for the augmentation of various body areas are limited only by the imagination of the patient and the skill and common sense of the surgeon. A wide range of procedures exists, covering most of the body, including cheekbones, pectoral muscle, calves, and buttocks. Few are very successful, and the most popular are for augmentation of bones such as cheekbones and chin.

The topic that leaps to mind when male body implants are mentioned is the **penile implant.** Penile implants or penis enlargements have attracted overwhelming interest, not limited to actual patients or even men, though much of this interest has now shifted to Via-

gra. The tabloid press and the men's magazines have made penile implants a more sensa-
tional issue than they should be. For the most part, the insertion of firm or inflatable silicon
struts is a well-regarded urological procedure for the treatment of male impotence. It is not
a procedure for penile enlargement.

The procedure for penile enlargement, called **phalloplasty**, is decidedly different and is
less well thought of within the medical community. Few men seeking penile enlargement
are actually smaller than the statistical range of normal, and those most qualified for the
procedure will find the least satisfactory improvement. Despite the fact that this is a procedure performed by few urologists, and fewer, if any, plastic surgeons, it is worthy of discussion if only to clear the air.

HAIR

It doesn't help a bit to remind you that fifty million other men have thinning hair. Nothing
makes it at all easier to accept. The pace of hair loss is predetermined and inexorable and
the end point is written in the genes. So why then, if it is so out of our control and so natural a life event afflicting so many men, do we take it so seriously? You won't find much of
the answer to that here. Anguish over hair loss is a fact so culturally ingrained and rein-
forced by movies, the media, and the cosmetics and pharmaceutical industries that we simply don't have a chance. Male vigor and virility are indelibly associated with hair. Full hair
is best, gray hair is okay, but thinning hair, and the specter of losing more, triggers reactions
out of proportion to the problem. Twenty-five, thirty, forty . . . it's happening . . . and men
change their hairdos, comb it, blow it, tease it, grow it, cut it, comb it over, and add all manner of lotions and potions to thicken what remains and disguise the loss. It is more than the
loss of hair, it is the loss of a state of mind inextricably intertwined with youth and virility,
so the combing and teasing is only the beginning.

For some men, hair loss slows along family lines, and they become resigned to what
seems a normal head of hair for early middle age . . . if only it will stay that way. For most
men the thinning look becomes acceptable at a certain stage of life. For the remainder, for
whom the process continues, male-pattern baldness is the eventual outcome.

It has been genetically determined that absent underlying illness, men who become bald
will do so in what is known as the male pattern. That is, the top, or crown, loses hair while
the sides remain unchanged. It is a situation few strive for, and many reach. Baldness is
inherited in an autosomal dominant pattern, with variable penetration. That means men

and women can inherit the tendency, but it doesn't always result in hair loss. There is an additional causative factor necessary for this pattern of baldness to occur, and that is the presence of circulating androgens, or male hormones. One must be unlucky enough to inherit the tendency, and virile enough to have enough circulating androgens to inhibit follicular activity. If it is any consolation, eunuchs do not exhibit male-pattern baldness. The old myth that baldness is inherited from the mother's side is just that, a myth. It is inherited without sex linkage from either parent, and in the presence of androgens, the gene does its dirty work.

Some deal with hair loss by shaving off what remains in a show of repudiation, or perhaps style. Others follow the trail begun with the initial loss, going the next step to hair-growing potions, hairpieces, and transplants. Others, perhaps the most emotionally healthy, ignore the whole matter. To these men I offer hearty congratulations. Hair loss changes nothing about a man but his hair. It signifies absolutely nothing beyond what you see, and if a man can deal with it casually, so much the better. If, however, you are among the majority who have given more than casual thought to the matter, you should at least be armed with the facts.

There are many ways to deal with and disguise hair loss. I will make no attempt to cover any but the medical elements. But having been a plastic surgeon for more than twenty years, and, I hope, an acute observer, I feel compelled to offer a few nonmedical comments.

In the quest to look good there is no substitute for a normal appearance. A caricature, any caricature, defeats the purpose of grooming and certainly of cosmetic surgery. You must insist on looking normal, and looking better. One of the many areas where this line is often crossed is hair. There is nothing natural, or the least bit attractive, about combing a few hairs from the sides of one's head over the bald pate. It looks silly, and it fools no one.

There are few hairpieces that don't look like caps. If you choose to go that route, get the best. Even they are often detectable. Many men have managed to come to grips with these facts about hairpieces and have made a weighed choice. There are public figures who appear with and without hairpieces, and treat the whole issue like the choice of clothing. "I'll wear it today—it goes well with my sporty outfit. Tomorrow I meet with the bankers, so I'll leave it home." Most of us would be unable to develop this sort of attitude, and perhaps it represents another form of defense mechanism, designed to ward off criticism before it occurs.

Other popular nonmedical techniques include hair weaving, and affixing hair to the scalp tied to metal anchors. In my view, hair weaving and related procedures have little to recommend them, for they rarely result in a natural appearance. Yet such techniques are a big business and many men seem satisfied with the result. Perhaps I'm being too picky. You be the judge. Is it easily detectable? Do you find yourself staring at the piece and not the person? If so, it just isn't good enough.

Growing New Hair

This should be the best solution to the problem, and we are periodically led to believe that the solution has been found. The most recent of these has been **minoxidil,** marketed as Rogaine. Clinical trials and practice have shown minoxidil to stimulate new hair growth, though the mechanism of this action remains unknown. It does this successfully in numerous disease states that have resulted in hair loss, particularly hormone-related states resulting in abnormal hair loss in women. It has also been reasonably successful in encouraging regrowth in women with thinning hair, as it has for some percentage of men using it to combat, or reverse, male-pattern baldness. Most estimates are that about 10 percent of male users report significant hair growth. Often this is in the form of very fine hairs, unlike the surrounding hair. On the bright side, one has hair where there was none. Within three months of the discontinuance of minoxidil usage, the new hair typically falls out. Still, for a certain percentage of users there is new growth, and under some circumstances it can be permanent.

Minoxidil is available over the counter, without prescription, in a solution of 2 or 5 percent. It is also available in higher concentration with a doctor's prescription. Used as a daily shampoo, it has few significant side effects, and it is not very expensive. Many men feel it makes sense to try the course and see what happens. I don't disagree. Don't expect too much and you won't be disappointed, and perhaps you'll be pleasantly surprised.

The actual cause for hair loss in male-pattern baldness seems related to the presence of receptors for the circulating hormone androgen at the hair follicle level, resulting in a local response at the follicle. The concentration of these **antiandrogen receptors** varies from the crown to the ring and from men to women. Predictably, more antiandrogen receptors are present in the crown, and there are more in men than in women. This theory is based on measurements of androgen and the hair growth response to blocking these antiandrogen receptors at the follicle. Much scientific effort is now being directed at making use of these findings. A French product based on local application of an antiandrogen blocker, labeled RU58841, is said to have been experimentally successful and to be not far from clinical trials.

The newest available drug therapy, and one that has shown great promise in clinical trials, is called Propecia, produced by Merck & Company. It has as its active ingredient **finasteride,** which has been marketed under the trade name Proscar for the treatment of enlarged prostate glands. Finasteride works by inhibiting production of dihydrotestosterone, the potent male hormone partially responsible for male-pattern baldness. Clinical trials following more than eighteen hundred men using the drug daily over a two-year period showed some improvement in 83 percent of cases. The extent of improvement varied from stopping hair loss to significant absolute increase in number of hairs per unit measured. In no case did a full head of hair regrow, but the results are impressive and the race is on.

Side effects from the one-milligram-daily dose of finasteride were predictably restricted to sexual dysfunction, since its action reduces production of male hormone. Fewer than 2 percent reported reduced libido, difficulty achieving erection, or decreased semen production, all of which reversed when therapy was stopped. But the use of finasteride is a lifelong commitment. When therapy ceases one can expect to lose the regrown hair.

An interesting sidelight to all this is that while Proscar contains a five-milligram dose of finasteride and Propecia only one milligram, urologists with wide experience following men using the higher dosage for enlarged prostates report very rare hair regrowth among their patients. This may be due in part to their paying very little attention to that part of the anatomy. Poor patient reporting may play a role, but that is unlikely, given how aware most men are about hair loss. Another explanation is that the drug stops hair loss but doesn't restore hair. One must also keep in mind that the Propecia study was conducted in a sampling of men from eighteen to forty-one, younger than the typical prostatic hypertrophy group, where hair loss has already occurred.

More studies and observations will surely be forthcoming, but for now the FDA has found the drug safe and effective for sale as a hair growth stimulant.

Minoxidil was a good first step, finasteride may be better yet, and scientists seem to be coming closer to understanding the balance between circulating male hormones and the response at the hair follicle level. This knowledge and the recent development of new compounds based on it have made the promise of an effective product to stimulate hair regrowth very real. The next several years will see more than one panacea evolve, but the ultimate outcome seems to have shifted to very hopeful. Despite all the hype and some good results, the use of minoxidil has not proved to be the answer for the fifty million men who might consider it. Finasteride will be the answer for an additional percentage, but with that

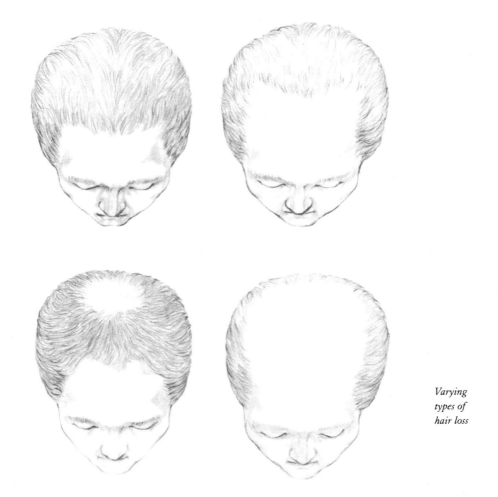

*Varying
types of
hair loss*

large a consumer base one can be certain that research is roaring ahead full tilt. They are close . . . but not quite there.

What, then, is the next step? For most, the hair loss was worrisome enough to consider some miracle potion that cost little in time and money, had few side effects, and seemed worth a try. The majority of men in the hair-thinning group will shrug off disappointment and take no further steps. The remainder of the group, men who have more significant hair loss or see thinning at any stage as the prelude to hereditary male-pattern baldness, or men who simply take it more seriously, will look further.

Hair Transplantation

This is the next step. This is a procedure that has been the mainstay of hair replacement for more than thirty years. In fact, it is the only reliable, permanent method of hair replacement available. It is not perfect, but it is the best we have to offer.

The actual procedure takes many forms, all related to the basic fact that male-pattern baldness spares the ring of hair around the sides and back of the head. The objective, therefore, is to transplant hair from areas of abundance to areas in need. There is no new hair growth, only redistribution of the wealth.

The average head contains a hundred thousand hairs. Under normal conditions some one hundred hairs are lost daily in the natural physiology of the scalp. These hairs regrow, and do not represent balding. However, decade by decade the number of active hair follicles is reduced significantly. This is so even in men who do not demonstrate male-pattern baldness. When hair loss is accelerated, the density in the area of loss reaches a critical point at which it becomes noticeable. This always happens at the top of the head in the area we call the crown. It may vary from crown to back among individuals, but it is always on top, never in the ring. Therefore, the objective of hair transplantation is to redistribute enough hairs from the permanent ring to the thinning crown to disguise the loss and provide lasting coverage. Nothing more.

The basic procedure was first popularized in the early 1960s, using the success of simple skin grafting as a template, the concept being free movement of small pieces of tissue to an area rich enough in blood supply to sustain the tissue's viability. There are numerous technical considerations, learned only by trial and error, which extended the rules of free tissue transfer beyond those of skin grafting. These were based on the nature of the recipient area, in this case the richly vascularized scalp, that allowed grafts of various shapes up to five millimeters in width to survive. A circular punch graft five millimeters in diameter contains approximately ten to twelve living hair follicles. The average full head of hair, as I have said, contains about one hundred thousand hairs. (Fair-haired people have about 30 percent more hair than dark-haired people, redheads 10 percent less.) Therefore a single hair plug transplants only one ten-thousandth of the scalp population, a very tedious process indeed. One can easily understand why some five hundred plugs may be necessary to make significant inroads against baldness. Five hundred plugs at ten hairs per plug delivers five thousand hairs, or 5 percent of the total hair on the scalp.

The underlying procedure has gone virtually unchanged in recent years. The bald, or balding, area is mapped and a plan for replacement is devised. This can include the use of plugs, micrografts, and strips, all of which are forms of transplants, and all based on the principle described above. The type of transplant used in a particular situation is chosen for reasons of coverage and aesthetics, with the goal of producing an attractive and natural appearance. As anyone who cares to look around can attest, this is easier said than done, but more about that later.

Plugs are the round grafts. These are taken with a round graft knife of the designated diameter. A slightly smaller plug is taken from the bald recipient site and discarded. The five-millimeter hair-bearing plug is then "stuffed" into the four-millimeter recipient site, where it remains firmly lodged, and in contact with the blood supply of the scalp. There it will flourish and continue to grow hairs, oblivious to the fact that it is now living in the previously bald area and not the sacred hair-bearing ring. A similar scenario applies to the

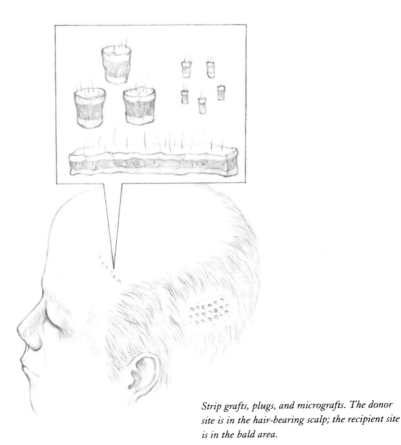

Strip grafts, plugs, and micrografts. The donor site is in the hair-bearing scalp; the recipient site is in the bald area.

micrografts. They differ from standard plugs in size, shape, and the number of hairs contained. Micrografts are placed between plugs to soften the appearance of the plugs against the scalp and help the transplanted hair blend in. As all of us are aware, the blending in is not always perfect. Hair strips are just that—strips of hair-bearing scalp harvested from the nonbalding ring, to be transplanted into the bald scalp. Strips take many shapes dictated only by a width of five millimeters and a sensible length that will be easy to work with and aesthetically pleasing.

The step-by-step process has also changed little over the years. The procedure is easy to perform, and more important, very easily tolerated. It is universally done as an outpatient procedure, under local anesthesia with, usually, supplementary sedation. The hair and scalp are cleaned, and with the patient in the sitting position and sedated, both the donor and recipient areas are infiltrated with lidocaine, a local anesthetic. This takes some ten minutes to achieve both numbing and temporarily reduced vascularity, accounting for the minimal bleeding incurred at the surgery. The hair of the donor site, usually toward the back of the permanent ring, is clipped short to be manageable and to show the natural direction of the hair growth. The objective is to put the hairs in their new site oriented in the proper direction according to the type of hair loss and surrounding direction of hair growth, among other considerations. These hairs are then harvested in the form of four- to five-millimeter-diameter plugs, using a hand-turned punch or an electric drill fitted to accommodate the hair punch, speeding things up considerably. In either event the process is painless. A similar number of slightly smaller circles are punched into the bald area and the skin discarded. The donor sites are allowed to heal, and they shrink in size over time. Initially, they are virtually hidden in the field of permanent hair within the ring and are not readily noticeable. As more plugs are harvested in succeeding sessions the donor area thins and the likelihood of the round, bald donor sites becoming visible increases.

Closure of the donor site is an area of difference among practitioners. If three hundred five-millimeter plugs are harvested from the ring along the sides of the head, the result will be three hundred small, round, bald scars. The more of these you have, the more noticeable they become. After a point the hair around these donor sites fails to disguise their presence, and a new defect has been created while correcting another. The donor sites do shrink somewhat, and careful planning within dense hair does a lot to make them less noticeable, but a checkerboard of bald circles has always seemed fairly unappealing to me. Some years ago, I published a scientific paper on a new method to harvest hair plugs and close the donor sites. The result was an interdigitated line that healed with far less visible mark than the plug pattern.

Oddly enough, though this technique was adopted by many plastic surgeons, the majority of hair transplant clinics are run by dermatologists, who have different ideas and a decidedly different level of surgical training. Whether they believe the effort to close the donor sites too time-consuming or simply unnecessary, they have neglected this option in droves. Still, it's there, and anything that makes the result more natural and aesthetically pleasing should be seriously considered. Most of the leading practitioners in the field now subscribe to some method of donor site closure.

In any case, the hair plugs and micrografts are prepared, oriented for direction of hair growth, and placed in the recipient sites. This does not require sutures and only an antibiotic ointment and firm dressing in the form of an elastic bandage are applied. The patient is discharged shortly thereafter, and returns over the next few days for dressing changes, and in a few more days for dressing removal. After two or three days, shower and shampoo are permitted, as the danger of dislodging plugs has passed.

The usual course is to implant one hundred to several hundred grafts per session, but more or fewer may be appropriate according to individual situations. Strips of hair-bearing scalp can be used for greater coverage, and micrografts may be inserted at this time, though usually this is done later in the course when it becomes more obvious where they are most needed. For a totally bald crown, several sessions are needed, and a minimum of five hundred plugs and micrografts may be necessary to achieve the goal. Thinning hair will require fewer, but things are in flux until hair loss stabilizes. Many men would prefer to get a jump on the situation in this way and not wait for actual baldness.

Over the next several weeks, the surface skin on the plugs sheds, along with the hairs that have been transplanted, leaving small pink circles that are quite noticeable, and quite bald. Most men wear a cap during this period, unless enough hair remains to disguise the new plugs. After twelve to sixteen weeks, new hair begins to sprout. This hair usually retains the characteristics of its source, and is permanent, so careful planning is imperative. After the new growth reaches sufficient length and can be styled, even if that means allowing it to lie uncombed over the scalp, it begins to do its job—coverage.

In the course of each session it will be apparent that a few of the plugs have failed to take, for a variety of reasons, and they can be replaced. Additional plugs and micrografts are inserted to achieve the most natural effect, and the process is complete.

The problem with hair transplants is that they are often instantly detectable. When this is the case, one is better off not having undergone the procedure, for little has been gained. There are many strategies to prevent this from happening, but they are not foolproof. There is always the risk that the plugs will be noticeable. If you can't deal with that, don't even consider the procedure. Sometimes hair transplants can be completely natural, and if not entirely undetectable, are not very noticeable. This is the sort of successful result every man, and every transplant surgeon, envisions.

There are several general rules that help predict the result, even before the surgery. Fair-haired men do better because there is less contrast between the new plugs of hair and the surrounding skin than in the case of dark hair. Remember, the plugs each contain some ten to twelve hairs. They cannot be placed against one another, as intervening skin is necessary to provide an uninterrupted blood supply. Therefore, in an individual with dark hair the circle of ten new hairs will stand out sharply against the surrounding skin. For this reason, micrografts, though time-consuming, yield a better result. Picture how much less obvious this would be in the case of light brown or blond hair. In dealing with dark hair it is important to place the plugs strategically and intersperse micrografts and single hairs wherever possible. Once the course is started in a dark-haired individual, it must be completed

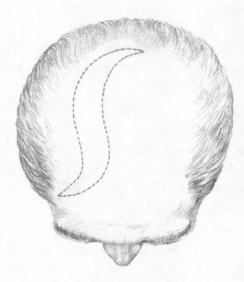

Scalp reduction: area of reduction

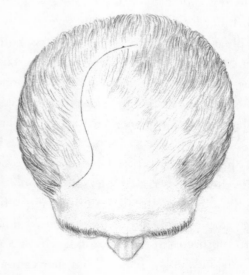

Scalp after reduction

in this manner to achieve the most natural result. "Natural" is the crucial word here, as in all cosmetic surgery.

Often, bald men are obsessed with having a full head of hair, in much the same way that truly flat-chested women often seek to have their breasts enlarged beyond what would be a natural result. In fact, their skin cannot naturally accommodate large implants and they must be satisfied with less than they dreamed of. So it is with baldness. A more natural result can be reached if one accepts an end point that looks like a thinning hairline, rather than teenage fullness. The more you push the envelope, the less natural the result.

Proper choice of end point, proper choice of donor sites, proper hair orientation, and completion of the full course all help achieve the best results. Hair transplants are expensive, often costing $5,000 to $10,000 per session, depending on the number of grafts. Typical sessions are two to three hours, as the work is tedious, and at least two sessions are usually required.

Other Procedures

Among the other procedures associated with hair replacement surgery is one known as **scalp reduction,** for reasons that will be obvious. The plan is to reduce the amount of bald scalp, thereby reducing the area requiring coverage and the number of plugs necessary. Weird as it may seem, it works. The operation is an easy one, and is performed under local anesthesia and sedation, as an outpatient. Utilizing a hyperbolic curve pattern, an amount of bald scalp that can be safely removed (and then closed) is excised. The scalp area is relatively pain-free and heals very well, thanks to its rich blood supply, making the procedure feasible. The bad news is that it is usually impossible to remove all the bald scalp, and a visible scar remains atop the head until it is fully surrounded with growing transplants. The cost is $3,000 to $5,000.

Utilizing **scalp flaps** to restore the anterior hairline is a more demanding technique but has many proponents within the plastic surgery community; it is a major surgical undertaking and beyond the surgical range of dermatologists. Here, large segments of hair-bearing scalp elevated from the ring along the sides of the scalp are rotated onto the front of the scalp, where they create a new hairline.

The procedure works because the flaps are based on sizable blood vessels that maintain their viability in the new position. It is fairly substantial surgery, and often several small surgeries in the postoperative period are required to achieve the finished product. The

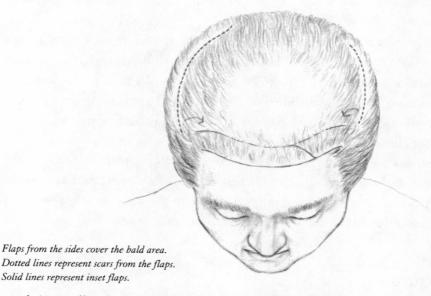

Flaps from the sides cover the bald area.
Dotted lines represent scars from the flaps.
Solid lines represent inset flaps.

result is usually a luxurious, full hairline. Unfortunately, the presenting edge is the surgical scar, followed by dense hair, not at all like the gradual onset of most mature hairlines. This can be dealt with by adding micrografts at the leading edge to soften the effect. Certainly this technique produces the fullest frontal hairline, but in my experience it is rarely natural, and a natural appearance, after all, is what we are trying to create. Is this technique better than hair plugs? I don't think so, but there are those who claim superb results. If this appeals to you, be sure to see examples of what your surgeon considers excellent results before you make the final decision. Fees average about $7,500.

The sticky issue in every method of hair replacement is the achievement of natural and unobtrusive results. This is not an easy task, and many men have been disappointed. You must know the facts and understand your individual case, your options and possibilities, in order to make an intelligent decision. For many, the prospect of baldness, in its many forms and degrees, is more disagreeable than a less than fully natural result. Others may reject this course. Some men need only filling out at the crown, and, as a rule, they will get satisfying results. Others will fare as well with full frontal transplants. Be sure you understand your own situation and your goals before making the decision to proceed.

Excess Body Hair

This is the other side of the coin. The two conditions, hair loss and excessive body hair, are not necessarily related, but they often coexist, increasing the clash of two extremes. The quantity and location of one's body hair is genetically determined, though it can be affected by a variety of drugs. Most often a rich growth on the chest, back, and shoulders creates a continuous pelt with the hair of the scalp at the back of the neck. Most men find this growth objectionable, but learn to live with it. Others shave, use depilatories, undergo electrolysis, and more recently have turned to laser hair removal. Each modality has its drawbacks.

Shaving is time-consuming and temporary, and regrowth is often quite annoying. Depilatories are temporary as well, and often irritating to the skin, though the results are smoother and closer than shaving. Electrolysis offers permanent hair removal. Unfortunately it is a tedious, uncomfortable process requiring destruction of individual hair follicles with low-grade current. The idea of treating the entire back and shoulder area with electrolysis is daunting to say the least.

Laser hair removal is the latest in superhype. As of this writing, none of the laser hair removal systems produces permanent results. The procedure is not very painful. It is quick, and large areas can be treated in each session. The results are fairly long-lasting, but the hair does regrow. The procedure is also expensive. The machine itself is very costly. Add to that office expenses, the cost of advertising for many of the clinics trying to establish position, and profit margin, and you can see how this temporary hair removal can cost thousands of dollars each year, usually $500 each session.

There is talk of new generations of lasers doing the job better and permanently. Thus far none has lived up to this standard. If you are interested in the process, be certain to ask questions. And remember—"long-lasting" does not mean permanent.

Hair Coloring

Why do you think so many women have excellent, healthy hair color when they should be gray, and men have hair that glows red in the light? Part of the reason is that more women avail themselves of professional help, but that can't be all. Many women color their hair at home; most men are victims of a wife's or girlfriend's good intentions. Still, the women look good and the men look silly. A lot is in the color choice. Women add all sorts of color and streaking, men seek only to cover gray and revert to the former color. Why, then, does the hair always look orange, or like a black cap?

I posed the question to New York hair colorist Beth Minardi. She pinpoints the cause as the use of "permanent" hair-coloring agents containing ammonia or ammonia substitutes, which allow an underlying hair pigment called phaeomelanin to surface. This pigment reads as a brassy reddish orange. This becomes increasingly obvious with ultraviolet exposure and shampoo, and soon sends the poor chap back to the bottle for more color, which only makes the result more artificial-looking.

What about the heavily advertised rinses to wash away the gray? As most men have noted, the results vary from man to man, and seem to change with time. The reason for this is said to be the metallic agents used, which denature with time. I'm not certain this is the cause, but so many men using these products look like men using these products—that is, they look unnatural. Newer products are nearing the market that should be far more effective, natural-looking, and long-lasting.

There are proper pigment combinations designed to minimize gray without bringing out the orange, and natural colors that aren't black as paint. But even when professionally done, the attempt to cover gray is a tricky business. If you are going to try it, find the best colorist, and be the most severe critic of your own appearance. No one cares as much as you, and no one has as much at stake. If it doesn't look perfectly natural, change colorists or give up the idea. There is no excuse for looking silly when you have a choice.

LIPOSUCTION

"Body sculpture" is the term frequently applied to liposuction, and that tells much of the tale of its popularity. Technically, the phrase is not quite accurate, but the picture it paints is very seductive. "Body sculpture" teases our self-images into focusing on the weaknesses we perceive in ourselves, holding out a magic bullet for their correction. Through lack of discipline or for other reasons, we are unable to effect the changes we wish. Then just as we were about to throw up our hands in resignation, as so many generations before have been forced to do, along comes body sculpture. Body sculpture, which in reality is no more than liposuction, is a process by which areas of excess fat are permanently removed from the body.

Liposuction was introduced to American plastic surgery in 1983. It had been used successfully in Europe for several years before the first groundbreaking article was published here. Fifteen years later, it is performed more frequently than any other cosmetic surgery procedure. Often part of other operations, it is performed by plastic surgeons and non–plastic surgeons alike, making accurate compilation of annual figures impossible. Some estimates list the use of liposuction as a primary procedure at about 150,000 instances annually. Somewhere beyond double this figure would reflect those procedures performed by physicians other than plastic surgeons and the use of liposuction as a secondary procedure, which would not ordinarily be reported. Some 25 percent of these patients are men, whose areas of concern differ significantly from those of women. Most often this means diet-resistant areas of fat accumulation such as "love handles," the waist, and the belly. Liposuction also miraculously eliminates the double chin and jowls, and can do much to reshape the body from the cheeks to the ankles, including the breast area. But it has its limitations and complications, and we will consider them as well.

Liposuction is based on the supposition that one is born with a specific number of fat cells in particular areas of the body. Though the fat cells may expand and contract with weight gain and loss, the actual number of cells per square inch doesn't change. Therefore, if you are at or about your optimal weight and you still have saddlebags of fat around your waist or a potbelly, you presumably have a greater number of fat cells per square inch of the overly large area than you have elsewhere on your body. The most sensible solution would be to remove fat cells where they are in excessive supply. This would roughly even out the distribution, and when you gain or lose weight, you would do so in a symmetrical fashion. Theoretically, when you gain weight the area would enlarge only in proportion to the rest of your body. And once the "love handles" are gone, they are gone forever.

This is the theory behind liposuction, and it works. For the last decade and a half, since liposuction was imported from France, we have continually refined our techniques, but the concept remains as simple as stated above. The removal of fat cells is accomplished by insertion of sterile steel catheters of various calibers into the area in question. The fat is then sucked out under high-vacuum tension. Crude as it may sound, that is what is done. It works, and it works well. Various forms of anesthesia are employed for the procedure, depending on the location, the extent, and the desires of the patient. It makes most sense to discuss details pertaining to each area, but in general the current trend is toward use of sedation, local anesthetics such as lidocaine, and the introduction of a tumescent solution in fairly large volumes. This refers to the use of a mixture of physiological saline, local anesthetic, and epinephrine, which is injected into the site, causing it to expand under the pressure. This physical expansion, in combination with the local anesthetic and epinephrine, serves to anesthetize the area quite effectively and facilitate the easy and bloodless removal of fat. For these reasons, in all but the most delicate areas, tumescent liposuction has become the rule. Some areas, like the face and jowls, require more precise planning and controlled fat removal and the tumescent technique is not used.

Ultrasound-assisted liposuction, UAL, is the newest development in the quest to remove ever-increasing amounts of fat with the fewest side effects. In this technique, fat cells are liquefied by sound waves, making removal easier and virtually bloodless. UAL has been touted as the second coming by those manufacturing and marketing the machine and the procedure. Unfortunately, virtually every careful study finds significantly less to rave about. UAL takes twice as long to perform as tumescent liposuction. This is because the equipment requires a straight-line approach to each area. More and larger incisions are required, and there is a far greater likelihood of injury to the skin. UAL does make the removal of vast amounts of fat possible, but this too is a mixed blessing. Dangerous complications, including the rare death, usually accompany removal of huge amounts of fat, because the electrolyte balance of the body is upset, or fat embolus (a globule of fat lodging in the lungs) may result. In liposuction of any type, the incidence of serious complications rises with the volume of fat removed. The final results are far from in, but massive fat removal by UAL, or by any other means, seems ill-advised. Particularly as very obese individuals are rarely in the best physical condition, extreme obesity is best treated by gradual weight loss, which allows the body to maintain homeostasis.

The best applications of liposuction are in the removal of fat deposits in genetically stubborn areas in minimally overweight individuals, but the possibilities are legion. Decisions regarding amount and areas should be made by the patient and his surgeon.

Microsuction, or the delicate liposuction about the face, has been discussed in the section on antiaging procedures. However, microsuction techniques can also be appropriate for heavy faces, double chins, and jowls in younger men in whom they are not related to aging but are simply inherited characteristics, as can be proved by perusing the family album. Here the results of microsuction are dramatic. The skin is still resilient and elastic and rapidly shrinks into shape, eliminating the need for actual surgery. For most men under the age of forty-five, microsuction is all that is necessary to permanently eliminate a double chin or jowls. Sometimes this procedure alone is effective at fifty or so, but there is always the chance that some loose skin will result, requiring surgical removal. Again, the younger the man, the better the result.

Other than the face, the most frequently treated area in men is the **love handles.** These are the soft areas above the hips and beneath the rib cage. They may be anything from a hint

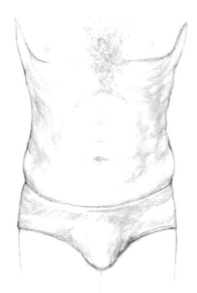

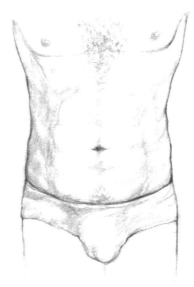

*After liposuction for
love handles*

Love handles

of excess tissue to a flabby roll. Love handles are sometimes continuous with a bit of fat across the belly, and they are most prominent toward the back, in the area one would call the flank. The problem is ubiquitous. It develops in early adulthood and worsens with age. In my experience, the fittest of men may have at least some suggestion of love handles. This being the case, one must concede that love handles are a fairly natural phenomenon, virtually uncontrollable without surgical help. Even with strict weight control and heavy exercise, most men seem to develop the condition to some degree. The point at which one calls it a problem is very personal, but in this age of exercise and hard bodies, I see more and more strong young men wanting to correct what would have been previously accepted as the norm.

The anatomical explanation of love handles is not clear. To some extent the condition is related to fat cells and fat accumulation. This happens in a typical male pattern; for genetic and hormonal reasons it occurs in males beyond adolescence and is rarely seen in women. It increases with age, probably because of a developing laxity of the oblique muscles, which make up much of the substance of the flanks. Add to this some weight gain and some predisposition to extra fat cells in the area and you have the conditions for the formation of love handles.

The treatment is liposuction. It is performed under heavy sedation or epidural anesthesia, which involves the temporary numbing of the spinal nerves. The method of choice depends on the wishes of the patient, plastic surgeon, and anesthesiologist together. What-ever the sedation or anesthesia chosen, the tumescent solution technique is usually employed as well.

Tiny incisions about a third of an inch long are made in an unobtrusive area toward the back, one on each side. The same incisions are utilized for the introduction of tumescent solution as for the actual liposuction. Varying amounts of fat are removed. The ultimate success of the procedure is closely related to the tone of the oblique muscles and the elastic-ity of the skin. Naturally, men with better muscle tone can expect better results. Still, it is impossible to remove the fullness totally. The results from liposuction of the love handles are rarely perfect but are uniformly good, and very much appreciated by patients. It is among the more popular procedures for men, particularly younger men for whom little else has so far changed with the years.

Liposuction of the abdomen is also quite popular among men of all ages. It is most suc-cessful among men who are in generally good shape, not massively overweight, and with-out loose skin. The factor limiting the amount of fat to be removed is the condition of the skin. Young, elastic skin allows more latitude, as it will rapidly shrink to fit the abdomen. In men of middle age and beyond, one must be alert to the possibility of reaching an end point of fat evacuation that results in loose, ill-fitting skin. This virtually negates the intended purpose; it merely exchanges one unsightly condition for another. Often when treating men of fifty or more I make it clear that common sense dictates ceasing fat removal before the point of exhausted elastic capacity. Determining that point is an arbitrary deci-sion based on the experience of the surgeon. To my mind, loose abdominal skin is more unsightly and aged-appearing than the preoperative state. Most men want every drop of fat removed and lose sight of the reality of the situation. It is very easy to keep going until all mobilizable fat is sucked out, and that is often the mistake of inexperienced and untrained operators. The abdomen requires the maintenance of its normal subcutaneous fat to look normal, as does virtually all of the body. Remove it, particularly in the face of reduced tis-sue elasticity, and the patient has not been well served. Removing too much fat or removal too close to the skin results in irregularities and dimpling of the skin. It is difficult to tread the fine line between achieving the goals of liposuction and the inherent pitfalls, and one must not lose sight of common sense.

The same anesthetic choices apply as for liposuction of love handles. In fact, the pro-cedures are often performed together. The tumescent solution technique is usually employed, and the postoperative course includes an abdominal binder and several days of limited activities. As with liposuction in other areas, there is minimal postoperative pain. In this area there is usually a sense of discomfort related to bruising of the abdominal muscles, not unlike any other muscle injury. Swelling and discoloration can persist for weeks, so one should not plan a seaside vacation immediately after the procedure. The customary counsel is not to expect to see much improvement for four to six weeks, because blood, tissue fluid, and tumescent fluid must be absorbed before softening and shrinkage can occur.

The complications of abdominal liposuction, in addition to loose skin, are puckering (which usually results from suction too close to the skin), irregularities, size disparities from side to side, and hematoma from injury to a blood vessel. That the latter happens so infrequently is a surprise to all surgeons who have seen the rich vasculature of the area firsthand. All sorts of unusual complications have been reported, such as perforation of the bowel and other internal disasters, but these situations are not related to the procedure but to the person performing it. Liposuction has a remarkably low complication rate in the hands of experienced operators. However, many untrained and reckless individuals perform this popular and remunerative procedure. Like all other cosmetic surgery, this is not an emergency, and one should select a surgeon carefully. It is better not done than done poorly. The fee range for liposuction varies with the area and volume in question. Most liposuction of the abdomen or love handles costs $5,000 to $7,500.

ABDOMINOPLASTY

Abdominoplasty, commonly referred to as the tummy tuck, is the operation necessary when loose skin or weak abdominal muscles are the problem. It was designed to eliminate the apron of fat and loose skin often seen after great weight loss in formerly obese individuals. Here there is too much excess tissue to be removed by any means other than surgery. This operation predates the advent of liposuction; it was once the only means available to remove excess fat from the abdomen. As the technique became more commonplace and surgeons became more comfortable with it, its applications expanded to its position as a proven and effective treatment, often performed in concert with liposuction.

The abdominoplasty incision runs horizontally across the pubic area just above the level of the pubic hair. This is the site of a natural skin crease, and the scar becomes reasonably invisible with time. The length of the incision varies with the extent of work to be per-

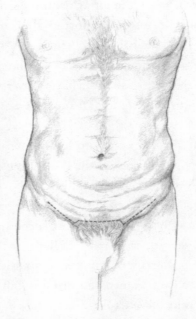

Incision for abdominoplasty

formed. Often it runs from hip to hip, but less extensive modifications are often appropriate. The incision allows the abdominal skin to be fully lifted off the underlying muscle, redraped, and trimmed, if that is necessary. Usually, the umbilicus (belly button) is moved to a new site after the skin excision. It is quite usual to excise all the skin from the umbilicus down to the pubis.

The primary muscles of the abdominal wall are the paired rectus abdominus muscles, coursing vertically from rib cage to pubis on either side of the midline. These muscles become weak and flaccid from lack of exercise or obesity. After elevation of the skin and fat from these underlying muscles and before closure, the abdominoplasty includes tightening these muscles, as well as removing excess fat, with or without liposuction, and removal of redundant skin. The package yields a firm, slim, taut abdomen, with the side benefit of decreased waist size. All this does not come without a price. The operation, while not entering the body cavity, is nonetheless fairly extensive. It takes approximately two hours to perform, and at least two weeks of recovery are required before resuming normal activities. Exercise and athletics can be resumed three weeks after surgery. There is considerable discomfort associated with the first few postoperative days. This takes the form of soreness, as one would feel with a muscle bruise, and a sensation of tightness, which is exacerbated by the postoperative swelling. All this abates in a few days.

After the postoperative period, the most annoying aspect of the procedure is the scar. Though it appears as a fine line early on, it soon thickens, rises, and itches. It takes at least a year for the scar to mature and for these symptoms to abate. With time the scar becomes soft, flat, skin-colored, and symptom free.

With the advent of liposuction, abdominoplasty is performed less frequently than in the past. However, individuals with considerable excess fat and fairly loose skin usually require both liposuction and abdominoplasty for the best result. Loose abdominal skin requires surgical tightening, or abdominoplasty, not liposuction.

Fees for abdominoplasty average $7,500 to $15,000.

RHINOPLASTY

Rhinoplasty is the surgical reshaping of the nose. Accurate as the term may be in medical jargon, many physicians have begun referring to the procedure as nasoplasty, which makes a lot of sense. It has been performed for most of this century, and results have improved steadily over the years. The operation is usually directed at overly large or misshapen noses, but often includes building or straightening nasal structure and restoration of internal nasal function.

One reason the operation is so widely accepted is that the actual surgery is usually performed through the nostril aperture and doesn't require external incisions. In some circumstances, like nostril reduction or reducing overly large nasal tip projection, external incisions become necessary. But they heal well and become barely visible in a very short time. Given all this, one wonders about all the awful "nose jobs" walking the streets. Perhaps they are just the few failures among the millions of successful nasoplasties performed over the years. For reasons of experience, skill, and aesthetics, rhinoplasty is among the most difficult procedures to master, and many practitioners have not done so. Physicians performing nasal surgery include plastic surgeons, otolaryngologists, and partially trained surgeons alike. Small wonder results vary so greatly.

The operation takes less than an hour to perform and is done in an ambulatory or hospital setting, under intravenous sedation and either local or general anesthesia. Recovery time from surgery until return to work is about a week. At three weeks, full physical activities may be resumed. Postoperative pain and discomfort are minimal after the first twenty-four hours. Swelling recedes rapidly, some 75 percent by the end of the first week, though the full resolution and ultimate result are not seen for several months.

Most men choosing nasal surgery for cosmetic purposes have it performed as young adults. Happily, the current aesthetic goal is to make it natural, which I find an excellent attitude.

Photographs of the patient are reviewed and altered and a reasonable understanding of expectations can be shared before surgery. This is invaluable communication and helps allay fears and prevent disappointment.

Often a large nose or a nose with a significant bony hump seems more prominent because of a weak chin. When this is not the case and a man has a strong jawline, he may be able to carry a large nose handsomely. When there is a relative imbalance it is not uncommon to enlarge the jawline with a **chin implant** at the time of nasal surgery. The implant is placed through the inside of the lower lip, below the teeth, and sits on the natural bone of the chin, making it project a bit farther. This simple maneuver allows the surgeon to perform less reduction of the nose in order to achieve the desired effect. The point of the exercise is a balanced profile and a nose of normal size and shape that doesn't detract from one's appearance.

As middle age approaches, many men seek nasal surgery with a slightly different complaint. With the passage of time the soft tissue of the nose accedes to the tug of gravity and descends. The tip of the nose seems larger as it stands away from the infrastructure, and it begins to point downward. This is particularly obvious when smiling. Bone is not affected by gravity in this manner, but soft tissue and the cartilage within the nasal tip drift downward, making the nose longer, the tip larger and lower, and the bony hump more obvious. What was acceptable and unremarkable in youth becomes something of an eyesore as middle age approaches, and many men are disturbed by the changes. Correction requires little more than reshaping the cartilage of the tip and restoring it to its former position. The small change effected achieves a more pleasant and youthful appearance without significantly altering one's overall appearance. This being the case, a tip plasty is often performed with face-lift and other antiaging surgery.

The goal in cosmetic nasal surgery is to produce a harmonious balance of features. This means different things in different cases, but one must not lose sight of the point of the whole thing: natural, balanced features. The idea of sticking a petite, turned-up nose in the center of a large masculine face is outrageous. In this operation, more than in many others, it is imperative to be conservative in one's approach and sensitive to the surrounding features.

The fees for nasal surgery average $5,000 to $10,000.

EAR SURGERY

Ear surgery is not high on the list of frequently performed cosmetic surgery procedures. It is worth noting because it falls into two categories: congenital deformities and changes caused by aging. The first is far more obvious, though much less common a problem.

The distance ears stand away from the head is genetically determined. In some families, and indeed in some societies, including a few counties in Ireland, it is the norm to have ears that stand away from the head like teacup handles, or **cup ears.** In other places protruding ears are a source of childhood teasing and derision. The teasing of children is intense. It is hurtful and not soon forgotten. Parents are aware of this, and often wish to have the problem corrected as early as possible. The majority of ear growth is completed in early childhood, and often the prominent ears appear oversized on the face of a boy five or six years old, who doesn't have the camouflage of long hair to hide behind. The fact that the ear cartilage growth is nearly completed makes it possible to perform the surgery in childhood. The usual course is to do the operation as close to the start of school as possible, as that is when the teasing begins. In other cases the operation is sought in teenage years or later.

The procedure itself is designed to re-create the natural back fold, or antihelix, in the ear and bring it closer to the head. This is done via an incision behind the ear, which heals quickly and well. Aside from a painful night or two, the major complaint is the need to

Left: cup ear. Right: creation of antihelix.

wear a headband to sleep for weeks in order to prevent accidental injury before full healing. Fees for such surgery average $7,500.

The other, more common, ear deformity is **stretched earlobes,** resulting from the pull of gravity on the earlobe. The earlobe is composed primarily of skin, fat, and blood vessels, and has little in the way of support. As a result of the constant pull of gravity, and perhaps years of inadvertent tugging, the earlobe stretches.

The elongated earlobe has an instantly aging look, not unlike the descent of the tip of the nose with age. Combined with fat redistribution and loss of skin elasticity it makes the ears look larger and seem to dominate the face. This can be corrected simply by removing a wedge of tissue and reconstructing the lobe. The operation is a simple one that can be done quickly under local anesthetic. It is virtually painless, and the scars diminish rapidly. Often this procedure is performed with face-lift or other antiaging surgery. The change is subtle and the overall result is excellent. Fees for earlobe reduction average $3,500.

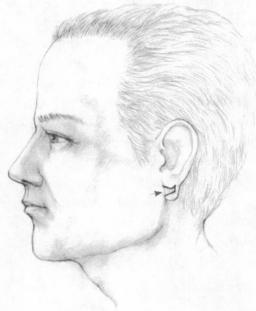

Stretched earlobe and diagram of reduction by removing a wedge of stretched tissue

GYNECOMASTIA

Gynecomastia is enlargement of the male breast. Causes of this condition include hormone imbalance, often decreased testosterone production, anabolic steroid use, hormone therapy for cancer treatment, and genetic predisposition. There is an association, perhaps apocryphal, with heavy marijuana usage. The condition is seen frequently among pubescent boys. Here, a temporary enlargement of one or both breasts accompanied by discomfort is often the cause of visits to the pediatrician. This form of the condition resolves spontaneously with the passage of puberty.

The appearance of gynecomastia varies from abnormal prominence above the pectoral muscles to frank breast mounds. In most cases an enlargement of the actual breast tissue is made more prominent by accumulation of surrounding fat. Whatever the case, the result-

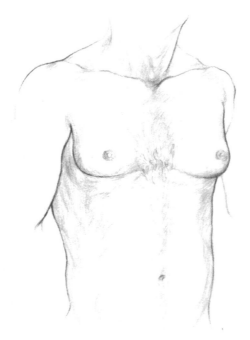

Gynecomastia

ing situation is embarrassing to men with the problem. It affects one's self-image and is a sore point dressed or undressed, among men or women, and is certainly a focal point when one is alone with the mirror.

Circulating hormonal stimuli tend to cause enlargement of both breasts simultaneously. Therefore, it is rare for only one breast to enlarge. This unilateral enlargement has been reported under a variety of circumstances, including among bodybuilders using anabolic steroids. Often unilateral enlargement argues for a local cause, such as a tumor or infection, but complete endocrine evaluation is the rule whether one breast or both are affected.

If the cause of gynecomastia can be ascertained, the first line of defense is removing the stimulus. In the case of hormone therapy, this obviously cannot be done. The removal of external causes, such as steroids, often results in some reversal of symptoms, but in the overwhelming majority of cases the cure is surgical.

The surgical procedure chosen to correct gynecomastia depends upon the anatomical elements. If the problem is an accumulation of fat, it can be treated very successfully with liposuction alone. This requires a tiny incision where the areola meets the skin, through which a liposuction catheter is inserted to remove excess fat. The perimeter of the fat removal is carefully tapered to blend with the surrounding tissue. When actual breast enlargement is present, as is usually the case, it must be surgically excised. This is performed through an incision along the areola/skin border as well, because of the nearly invisible scar that results in this location. The enlarged breast is of firmer consistency than fat and must be removed by surgically freeing it from the surrounding structures, including the underside of the nipple. Liposuction is then employed to blend the surrounding fat with the area, though sometimes the removal of large amounts of breast tissue may result in a defect at the site.

Postoperative swelling and discoloration are the rule, as it is difficult to adequately and comfortably compress the area. After a few weeks the improvement becomes obvious, and virtually every man who has undergone the procedure is happy to have had it done. The operation is performed in an ambulatory or hospital setting and under sedation and local anesthetic or under full general anesthesia. It takes about an hour to perform and costs between $5,000 and $10,000.

PENIS ENLARGEMENT

The truth now . . . did you go right to this section after noticing the topic in the contents? So much for "size doesn't matter." In truth, it probably does not, but perception is another reality altogether. Size and sexuality go hand in hand in the perception of both partners. Most men are average in penis length and circumference. That means different things to different observers. I made an effort to get specifics from several urologists, who not only couldn't supply the statistics but felt knowing the numbers would do more harm than good. Few sex partners complain about size. Some may have been accustomed to greater proportions, and a few have actually complained about a partner being too large. Most agree that except for extreme examples, most men are average, whatever that means, and performance is what counts. Still, there is no doubt that for some people an unusually large member will attract sexual interest, even if the size causes difficulties.

Even if it were worth doing, there is absolutely no way to effect enough size increase to make one very large. In fact, there is less than meets the eye in the whole matter of penis enlargement.

Those few genuinely small men seek help for psychosexual reasons. Self-doubt and diminished self-image outweigh functional reality. A number of procedures have been devised to increase penis size, and these are at the far edge of good medicine—not merely because they are unnecessary, poorly done, or done by untrained physicians, but because they rarely meet patient expectations. The procedures employed include incising the suspensory ligaments at the base of the penis, followed by months of stretching using weights attached to the penis. This gives new meaning to the term "weight training" and is said to stabilize the gain made by ligament resection. The release and subsequent weight therapy is said to allow up to an additional inch in length, occasionally more, in erect extension. This gain in length is paid for with a loss of upward positioning in the erect state, and often the presence of pubic hair on the base of the penis.

Additional width can be gained by transplanting fairly large volumes of fat into the shaft. Most of this is reabsorbed, because the volume injected cannot all come in contact with blood supply to sustain it. Therefore the size regresses significantly after six months. The fat that survives tends to do so in an irregular pattern, creating a thicker, lumpy penis. Another method for increasing penile width is dermal fat grafting. This technique employs the harvesting of strips of the dermal undersurface of the skin with its attached fat and transplanting it into the penis. This should offer longer-lasting results, but requires several external incisions of some size to harvest the dermis. It is more of an operation than fat injections, and complications such as bleeding and infection are more likely.

Most reputable urologists and plastic surgeons do not perform this procedure. They have seen or heard of the legions of disappointed, and sometimes deformed, men who wanted to be "bigger," and they feel the procedure does more harm than good.

The man who actually feels inadequate about his penis size is best advised to see his urologist before answering ads in the back of men's magazines. Exceedingly few men are truly deficient, and fewer still will actually gain significantly from this procedure.

Afterword

This survey has covered an enormous range of information aimed at helping today's man look his best well into the twenty-first century. A great deal of progress is being made on every scientific front, assuring unheard-of longevity and relative control over our appearance. Aging as we know it will be a thing of the past. For today we have much to work with as we watch the progress unfold. We each have different agendas, and we must sift through the facts and make some judgments regarding how much of the information offered applies to our individual lifestyles, and how much effort we are willing to expend to help ourselves.

Meanwhile, there are some basic strategies that work and that every man should incorporate into his life. They cost little, and offer a phenomenal upside of positive rewards. They are:

- Daily vitamins C and E
- Skin care routine
- Sunscreen
- Weight stabilization
- Dietary reform
- Exercise

This is simple stuff, not earthshaking lifestyle changes, or surgery. Perhaps a bit of effort and self-discipline might be necessary, but if you really care about how you look and how you feel, you have to start somewhere. Cosmetic surgery alone is not the answer, nor is growth hormone, nor will megavitamins and the marathon do the job. But there is much that can help, and we can't start without you. Whatever your stage of life, make today's science work while we all await the future.